JEWELRY STUDIO

WIRE WRAPPING

JEWELRY STUDIO

WIRE WRAPPING

Linda Chandler and
Christine Ritchey

INTERWEAVE.
interweavebooks.com

Interweave Press LLC
201 East Fourth Street
Loveland, CO 80537-5655 USA
interweavebooks.com

Printed in China by Asia Pacific Offset.

Library of Congress Cataloging-in-Publication Data

Chandler, Linda L., 1946-
 Jewelry studio : wire wrapping / Linda Chandler and Christine Ritchey.
    p. cm.
 Includes index.
 ISBN 978-1-59668-059-3 (pbk.)
 1. Jewelry making. 2. Wire craft. I. Ritchey, Christine R., 1951- II. Title.
 TT212.C4525 2008
 745.594'2--dc22
                        2007029450

10   9   8   7   6   5   4   3   2

CONTENTS

Welcome to the Jewelry Studio!

Welcome to the world of wire wrapping. In this book, you'll learn how to make a range of jewelry pieces, from some of the simplest to some of the most complex. Wire-wrapped jewelry, made with wire and beads, makes use of mechanical connections—there is no soldering involved in these techniques. Wire wrapping is an ancient art, dating back some 4,000 years to the Sumerian Dynasty. Wire-wrapped jewelry has also been found in ancient Roman digs. At the very least, this tells us that wire-wrapped jewelry must be very durable!

You won't find wire-wrapped jewelry in department stores. By its very nature, this jewelry is always handmade, and thus one of a kind. A well-made piece of wrapped jewelry will be treasured for many generations.

The techniques and projects presented here are yours to use as you wish. A good cook may follow a recipe exactly the first time and then decide to add more cinnamon or less curry the next time. The instructions in this book should be used the same way. They are not written in stone. (If they were, this book would be huge and way too heavy!)

A word about the Jewelry Police: We assure you that they exist only in your head. The Jewelry Police will tell you that your jewelry isn't good enough, or that you absolutely must follow the instructions in this book exactly. They pass judgements and ruin creativity. So tell those muttering voices in your head to zip it and feel free to add or subtract beads, change wire gauges, or use your own new idea for a clasp. Most importantly, have a sense of humor and have a good time making your jewelry.

As always, we're here to help. You'll find Christine's e-mail address in the back of this book, along with addresses for both of our websites. These sites are always works in progress, and we hope they'll provide you with further inspiration and information.

We sincerely hope that you enjoy using this book as much as we enjoyed writing it.

CHAPTER ONE

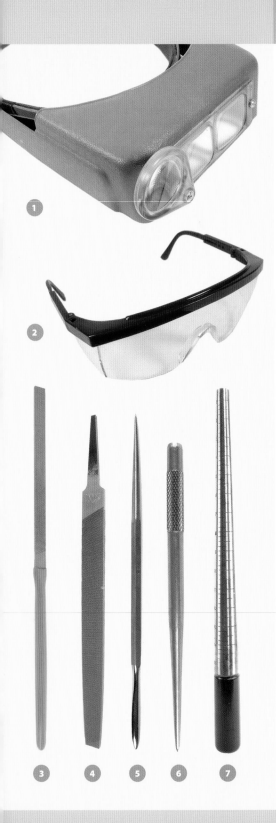

Tools and Materials

For some of us, buying cool tools is almost as much fun as making jewelry! Here is the equipment you'll need for all of the projects in this book, plus some nonessentials that you'll find helpful. If you're just getting started, inexpensive tools are available, but it's a good idea to buy the best quality you can afford. See Resources in the back of this book for good places to find tools.

THE ESSENTIAL TOOLS

1 **Opti-Visor:** An Opti-Visor or other magnifying glasses brings your work in close, reducing eyestrain and allowing greater precision.

2 **Safety Glasses:** These protect your eyes from flying debris and the stray ends of wires. Wear them all the time. They'll fit under the Opti-Visor, which does not offer full protection.

3 **Flat File:** A flat file has teeth on both sides and is used for smoothing wire ends and metal edges.

4 **Coarse File:** A coarse file will make the heavier filing required for the Patterned Wire Bracelet much easier.

5 **Scribe:** A scribe is used to mark metal in a pattern for cutting or sawing.

6 **Center Punch:** A center punch is used to make a small dent in metal or to flare the ends of wire used in a cold connection.

7 **Ring Mandrel:** You'll need a ring mandrel every time you make a ring or need to determine an existing ring's size. They come in several varieties: wood, metal, stepped, and tapered.

8   Rawhide Mallet: Use a rawhide mallet when forming wire around mandrels (see the Wire-Wrapped Ring) or to work-harden a metal shape without marring the metal.

9   Penknife: Use a penknife to pry and manipulate wires.

10 Pin Vise: A pin vise holds wires. Hold the other wire end with pliers and roll the pin vise along your thigh to make twisted wire.

11 Flush Cutters: Flush cutters cut wire without leaving a "point" in the cut wire. This reduces the amount of filing you'll need to do to make a smooth wire end.

12 End Cutters: End cutters are used to cut very heavy wire, such as the wire used in the Patterned Wire Bracelet. Jewelry catalogs will tell you what thickness of wire each set of pliers will cut. You can buy end cutters at a hardware shop and save a little money.

13 Nylon-jaw Pliers: Nylon-jaw pliers are great for forming wire without leaving marks, dents, or scratches. They're also great for straightening wire.

14 Chain-nose Pliers: Chain-nose pliers are among the most useful tools you can have. You'll use them for all kinds of wire-forming tasks.

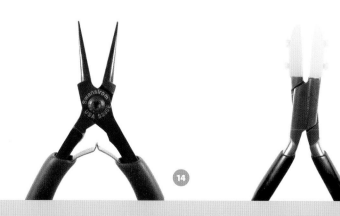

15 Round-nose Pliers: Round-nose pliers form loops and curves in wire.

16 Flat-nose Pliers: Flat-nose pliers are used to form, press, and hold wire.

17 Step-nose Pliers: These form varying sizes of loops and curves in wire.

18 Tumbler: A tumbler is essential for the final polishing of your jewelry. It removes light scratches and dings and imparts a uniform luster to metal surfaces.

Good To Know:

A hammer and steel bench block are used to harden wire and sheet metal by tapping the jewelry lightly several times. If you want to achieve a forged, hammered look, just hit the jewelry piece a bit harder until you achieve the look you want.

Dowels of varying sizes can be used in place of some pliers to make curves and loops and are very useful for making jump rings.

Masking tape holds wires together and can be wrapped around plier jaws to prevent marring of wire.

A ruler should be kept nearby to measure wire lengths.

Goo-Gone or acetone will remove the "glop" left behind when masking tape is removed.

A felt-tipped marker, such as a Sharpie, is used to mark measurements on wire.

COOL TOOLS
(NOT ESSENTIAL, BUT NICE TO HAVE)

Flat/Round-nose Pliers have one round jaw and one flat. They don't mar the wire as much as round-nose pliers.

Hemostats are great "third hand" helpers. Use them to hold wires together. They grip more tightly than masking tape, are adjustable, and are easy to use—very helpful in some situations. Caution: Many hemostats have serrated jaws that can mar your wire, so you may need to tape them before clamping.

Many file types are available, but one you'll find very useful is the **Barrette File.** These files have teeth on one side and are smooth on the other, allowing you to file in tight spaces without damaging adjacent metal.

The Wire Wrapping Ring Mandrel (which we call the **Step Mandrel**) provides common diameters around which wire can be bent and formed. It takes the place of several dowels or rods and is available in different sizes.

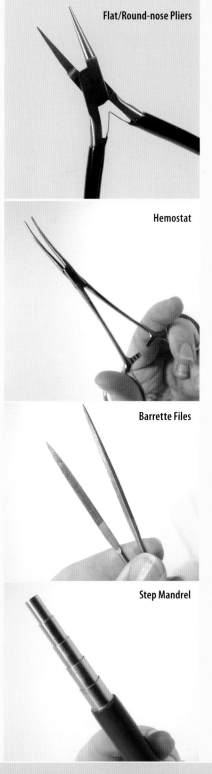

Flat/Round-nose Pliers

Hemostat

Barrette Files

Step Mandrel

THE ESSENTIAL MATERIALS

Shopping for wire and beads is one of the most fun things about making jewelry. Wire comes in all shapes and sizes. Beads can be fashioned from precious and semiprecious stones, Austrian crystals, pearls, and dichroic glass. There are many, many more kinds of beads, and all of them will call to you when you go into a bead store, look through a catalog, or shop on the Internet. Here we'll discuss the properties of wire and some of the many characteristics of beads.

WIRE

Wire comes in gold, sterling silver, fine or pure silver, gold-filled, copper, and brass. Of course, there are others, but these are the metals most often used in jewelry making. For wire wrapping, karat gold and fine silver are seldom used because of their softness. We'll concentrate on sterling silver and gold-filled wire, as these are the most common metals used in wire wrapping.

Temper

Temper is the degree of hardness or softness of the wire. Wire is available in dead-soft, half-hard, and hard tempers. Dead-soft and half-hard tempers are both acceptable for square wire, while half-hard is usually preferred for half-round wire.

Shapes

Wire comes in round, half-round, square, triangular, and double half-round. For the purposes of this book, we'll use half-round and square wire and a little round wire as well.

Gauge

In the United States wire size is measured in gauges. The largest gauges have the lowest numbers, such as 6-gauge; 26-gauge is a very fine wire. Europe and other parts of the world measure wire size in millimeters, so we have provided both gauge and millimeters when specifying wire size. At left is a chart showing some commonly used wire gauges.

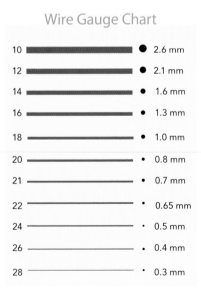

Wire Gauge Chart

Gauge	Diameter
10	2.6 mm
12	2.1 mm
14	1.6 mm
16	1.3 mm
18	1.0 mm
20	0.8 mm
21	0.7 mm
22	0.65 mm
24	0.5 mm
26	0.4 mm
28	0.3 mm

BEADS

Beads are always measured in millimeters. Since beads can be made of almost any material, they, too, are judged by hardness or softness. The Mohs Scale is used for this. Stones are rated from 1, the softest, to 10, the hardest. This is actually a scratch test. Talc, for example, is rated on the Mohs Scale as a 1. This means that its surface can be scratched by a finger-nail and by any other stone rated 2 or above on the Mohs Scale. Diamonds can scratch anything and are virtually impossible to scratch, so their rating is 10. What all this means is the higher the rating on the Mohs Scale, the more durable the stone will be.

Beads and stones are available in a vast range of cuts and sizes. Below is a millimeter size chart showing some of the most commonly available round sizes.

In addition, for the Stone Pendant on page 101, you'll find what is called a "slab" of rock. A slab is a piece cut from a larger stone with a lapidary saw and then shaped and polished with lapidary equipment. In the Stone Pendant project, you'll learn what to look for in a well-made slab. It's quite interesting, really!

Round MM Size Chart

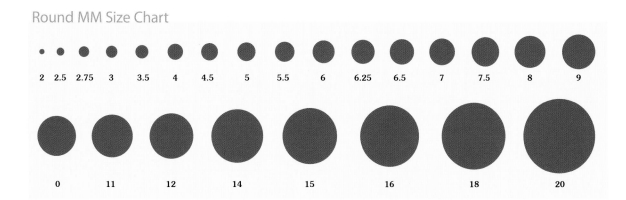

CHAPTER TWO

Wire Fundamentals

Safety is fundamental to jewelry making. Wire wrapping isn't very dangerous, but in this chapter we'll point out a few things to keep in mind for your own well-being and the welfare of your family. We'll also offer a few suggestions for getting the most out of your tools. A little care and effort will pay big dividends when making jewelry. Next, you'll learn how to make jump rings and why they're made the way they're made. We also offer a simple clasp that can be used with much of the jewelry in this book.

SAFETY FIRST

Wire wrapping is not a very hazardous activity, but there are a few things to be aware of.

◎ Guard your eyes from flying wire pieces during cutting by holding on to both sides of the wire to be cut. Don't depend on your magnifying glasses for protection. Wear safety glasses along with your magnifier. Every hour, take off your magnifier and look into the distance for a few moments to prevent eye fatigue.

◎ Repetitive hand motion can cause carpal tunnel syndrome. While you're looking off into the distance, make tight fists and then spread your fingers apart as far as possible. Do this several times. Place your hands one at a time on a sturdy flat surface. Spread your fingers and gently lean on your hand to bend your wrist.

◎ Keep children and pets away from your workspace. It's amazing how the most harm-less-seeming things can become dangerous in the hands of a small child or the mouth of an inquisitive dog.

◎ Protect your neck and back by working fairly close to eye level. Choose a comfortable stool or chair. Make yourself get up and walk around. (You can do this while you're resting your eyes and exercising your wrists.) Do some neck rolls and touch your toes.

◎ If you're tired, get a headache or a sore neck, or find that you're not having fun, stop making jewelry and go do something else.

◎ Finally, don't decide in October that you're going to make presents for everyone for Christmas or Hanukkah. You'll never make it, and you'll only add more stress to the holidays by trying. We speak from personal experience!

TIPS FOR GETTING THE MOST OUT OF YOUR TOOLS

USING A TUMBLER

We strongly recommend that you buy mixed stainless-steel shot to use in your tumbler. The non-stainless-steel shot is cheaper but is much more difficult to maintain.

Fill the tumbler barrel with shot and water according to the manufacturer's instructions. Also, add a polishing liquid such as Sunsheen or several drops of liquid dishwashing detergent. If the water in your neighborhood is very hard, using distilled water will prevent contamination of your stainless-steel shot.

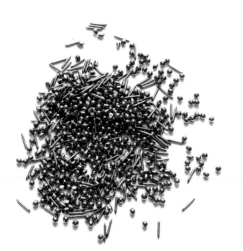

If your shot starts looking gray and dull, dump it onto newspaper and clean the barrel thoroughly. Rinse the shot in a wire-mesh colander and put it back into the barrel. Add burnishing liquid and water and tumble until the shot is shiny again. You won't need to do this often, but if your tumbled jewelry comes out looking gray and ugly, it will definitely be time to clean the shot. Once the jewelry is tumbled again, it will look nice and sparkly.

Yes, you can tumble jewelry that has beads or stones! Hard stones, such as cubic zirconias, can be tumbled without concern. For soft stones such as opals or shells, monitor the tumbler's progress carefully and limit the time the jewelry is in the tumbler.

Some people tumble their jewelry overnight. One to three hours is usually enough time to shine up your jewelry.

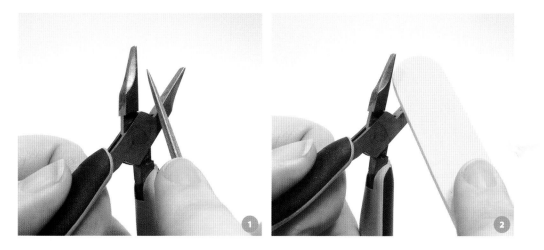

SOFTENING THE EDGES OF PLIERS

The hard, sharp edges on most pliers can damage your jewelry by leaving gouges, dents, and dings in the wire as you manipulate it. To minimize this risk, you can soften sharp edges by lightly filing and rounding them, first with a flat file **(Figure 1)**, then with an emery board to sand the edges smooth **(Figure 2)**.

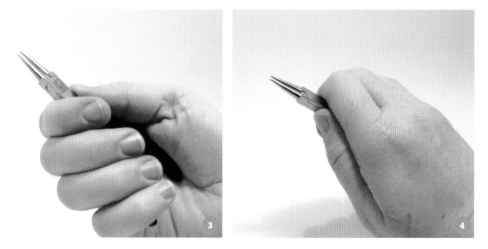

HOLDING PLIERS CORRECTLY

When starting to curl wire, hold the pliers with your palm facing upward, so you can see what you're doing. Rotate the pliers toward your body as you make the curl. You'll have greater control with your thumb near the jaws and all fingers grasping the handles **(Figures 3 and 4)**.

STRAIGHTENING WIRE

Wire comes either coiled or spooled **(Figure 1)**. One good way to straighten wire is to gently take the broad curves out with your fingers **(Figures 2 and 3)**. To smooth the smaller bends, hold the wire lightly with a pair of nylon-jaw pliers and pull the pliers slowly along the length of the wire **(Figure 4)**.

WIRE JEWELRY CARE AND MAINTENANCE

Avoid wearing wire jewelry in swimming pools and hot tubs; pool chemicals will turn silver black. The hairdressing salon and your own bathroom are not your jewelry's best friends, either. The chemicals used in hair care and to clean plumbing can damage silver's shiny surface.

When you're not wearing your jewelry, keep it in plastic zip bags to prevent tarnishing. If tarnishing occurs, use a good commercial jewelry cleaner. It has polishing agents that will help restore the luster to your jewelry.

Another alternative is to coat your jewelry with a sealant, such as Everbrite. This invisible coating will prevent oxygen and chemicals from reaching silver and gold-filled wire.

PRACTICE: Jump Rings

Jump Rings are used to connect various jewelry components. Sure, you can buy jump rings, but you can save money by making your own, and you can make them any size you want. They are also a good place to start getting comfortable with wire wrapping.

TOOLS AND EQUIPMENT
Flush cutters
Nylon-jaw pliers (for straightening wire)
Flat-nose pliers
¼" (6 mm) diameter dowel

YOU'LL NEED
About 8" (20.5 cm) of 16-gauge (1.3 mm)
  dead-soft, round, silver, or gold-filled
  wire

TIP: The dowel size and wire gauge we're using are just examples. In general, the larger the dowel size, the heavier gauge wire you'll need to use. The reverse is also true—to a point. Although lighter-gauge wire can be used with smaller dowels, the links will be weak if the gauge is too light.

Step 1: Straighten about 8" (20.5 cm) of wire. This length of wire should give you about 10 jump rings.

Step 2: Start wrapping the wire around the dowel (**Figures 1 and 2**). You'll have more control if you start the wrap several inches from the end of the wire or, as shown in this example, about in the middle of the wire.

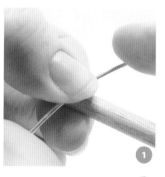

Step 3: The wraps should be as tight and even as possible. After a few turns, use flat-nose pliers to press the wire more firmly against the dowel **(Figure 3)**, then continue with more wraps.

Step 4: The pliers will be needed to finish the last turn. Finish winding, and use the flat-nose pliers to press the end of the wire smoothly against the dowel for a tight, even coil **(Figures 4 and 5)**.

Step 5: Remove the coil from the dowel. If the wire doesn't slide off easily, untwist it by turning the ends in opposite directions slightly and pulling the coil off the dowel at the same time.

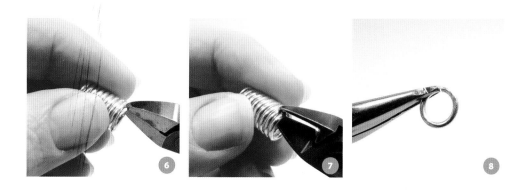

Step 6: Sometimes the first ¼" (6 mm) or so of wire isn't as perfect as the rest of the coil, so you can trim it off with flush cutters (make sure the flat side of the jaws is facing the coil **(Figure 6)**.

Step 7: Now you can cut the individual coils with the flush cutters, moving up the center of the coil **(Figure 7)**. Each turn of wire you cut becomes a jump ring **(Figure 8)**.

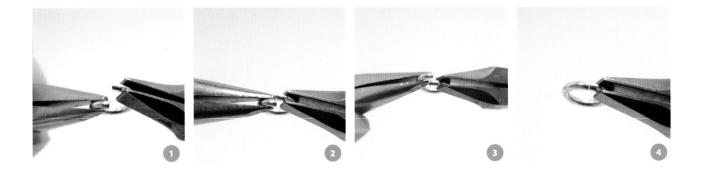

OPENING AND CLOSING JUMP RINGS

Step 1: The proper way to open a jump ring is by twisting the wire ends sideways—never pull them straight back (**Figure 1**).

Step 2: Close the link by pushing the wire ends past each other, first on one side (**Figure 2**), and then on the other side (**Figure 3**).

Step 3: Finally, bring the ends together, and you'll have a perfect closure (**Figure 4**)!

PRACTICE: Catch and Clasp

Here's a versatile catch-and-clasp arrangement you can customize for many wire-jewelry projects. The catch and clasp are relatively easy to make, can be of different lengths and widths, look great, and connect securely. Several projects in this book use this basic design. You can use a variety of wire gauges and shapes—round, square, or half-round—or mix and match, like we've done here.

TIPS: We used flat/round-nose forming pliers to create the clasp. These pliers can bend and curl wire without leaving damaging indentations. You can also use step-nose pliers.

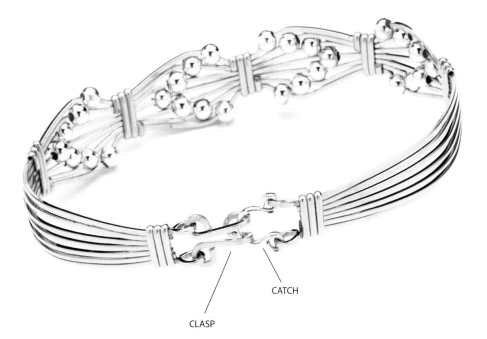

CATCH

CLASP

MAKE THE CLASP

Step 1: Straighten a length of the square wire, then cut off a piece 1¾" (4.5 cm) long. Trim any burrs and file both ends flat.

Step 2: Center the wire in the jaws of step-nose pliers, using the smallest step, and bend the wire into a U shape with your fingers **(Figure 1)**. If necessary, adjust the wires so that you have a balanced U shape that is equal on both sides **(Figure 2)**.

Step 3: Position the tip of the pliers at the end of the wire **(Figure 3)**. Maintaining a firm grip, rotate the pliers as far as your hand will allow. This will form a partial loop **(Figure 4)**.

Step 4: Reposition the pliers and bring the loop to a close **(Figure 5)**. Repeat on the opposite side. Both loops should match as closely as possible **(Figure 6)**.

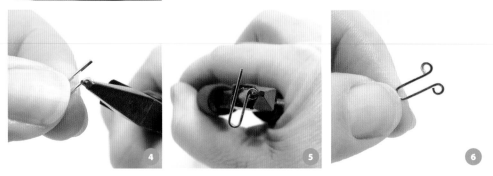

Step 5: Use flat-nose pliers to flatten and even up the loops **(Figure 7)**. Be sure to squeeze firmly for a successful flattening job **(Figure 8)**.

Step 6: While holding the loops firmly, use step-nose pliers to bend up the very end just a little, using the smallest diameter step **(Figure 9)**.

Step 7: Reposition the pliers so that the middle step is centered at the start of the bent-up part and curl the clasp into an L shape **(Figures 10 and 11)**.

Step 8: Now reposition the pliers to the smallest diameter step and continue curling the L until it becomes a U shape **(Figure 12)**. You will probably have to reposition your pliers again to complete the curl **(Figure 13** shows a completed curl).

TIP: What if you have an uneven curl? To cure this problem, hold the loop ends of the clasp with flat-nose pliers and use chain-nose pliers to flatten and straighten.

MAKE THE CATCH

Step 1: Cut a piece of 16-gauge (1.3 mm) dead-soft, half-round wire ⅞" (2.2 cm) long. Using a ³⁄₁₆" (5 mm) dowel or step mandrel, curve the wire into a U shape **(Figures 1 and 2)**.

Step 2: Using the smallest part of your round-nose pliers, bend the legs of the U in or out to make them even **(Figure 3)**. Then bend the two legs into an outward curl **(Figure 4)**. If the curls are crooked, correct with flat-nose and chain-nose pliers **(Figure 5)**.

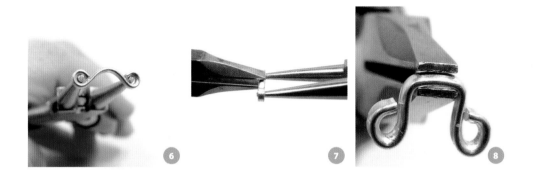

Step 3: After the piece is aligned, place it on the round-nose pliers **(Figure 6)**. While holding the piece with round-nose pliers, use flat-nose pliers to form the catch into a pleasing shape that will receive the clasp **(Figures 7 and 8)**.

CHAPTER THREE

Basic Projects

Just like learning in school, you need some basic skills before you get to study "the good stuff." Master the Basic Bracelet before moving on to more elaborate projects. Actually, the Basic Bracelet is very pretty and may well become a staple product in your jewelry making. Once you've mastered the Basic Bracelet, you'll build on the skills you've learned to make more complicated projects. The Celtic Knot Bracelet provides a small break from strictly wire wrapping. It's a fun project that gives you a very stunning piece of jewelry.

Basic Bracelet

This bracelet is the foundation for all the wire wrapping you will ever do. When you master this, all the other projects will be much simpler to make. So please make this bracelet first! These bracelets look great worn in threes. Try making two like the one described here and another using silver square wire with gold-filled wraps. Very elegant!

TIPS: If you're very picky about how your wraps look, perfecting them here will make the other projects so much easier. Use copper or brass or both to practice with, until your wraps are even. There is no magic formula, just practice, practice, practice. Be ruthless! If you can't fix a wrap, take it off the bracelet and try again with a new piece of half-round wire.

Save all your silver and gold-filled scraps. They can be sent to a refiner (see Resources) and exchanged for either money or new wire.

TOOLS AND EQUIPMENT

Flush cutters

Flat-nose pliers

Round-nose pliers

Chain-nose pliers

Step-nose pliers

Nylon-jaw pliers

Flat file

Penknife

Ruler

Hemostat (not necessary, but useful)

Felt-tipped marker

Masking tape

Acetone or Goo-Gone

YOU'LL NEED

About 42" (107 cm) of 20-gauge (0.8 mm) square, half-hard gold-filled wire

About 48" (122 cm) of 18-gauge (1.0 mm) half-round, half-hard sterling silver wire. (You may want to have more on hand to allow for mistakes.)

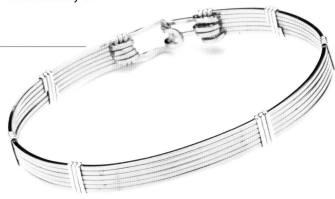

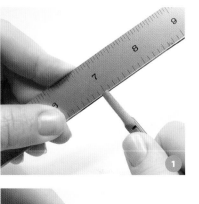

Step 1: Following the instructions in the Wire Fundamentals chapter, straighten all wire. For a 7" (18 cm) bracelet, measure and cut two pieces of square wire 14" (35.5 cm) long. Place flat-nose pliers at the middle of one wire **(Figure 1)**.

Step 2: Using your thumb and index fingers, bend the wire partially down along each side of the pliers **(Figure 2)**. Remove the wire from the pliers, turn it around, and replace it; then finish the bend. Reversing the wire in the pliers helps keep the wire lengths about equal.

Step 3: Square wire is very easily twisted. Make sure that the same side of the wire is facing upward all along the wire. Use flat-nose pliers to press the wire flat and even **(Figure 3)**.

Figure 4 shows the finished shape of the wire. This wire piece will become the bracelet frame, and the bent end will become the catch.

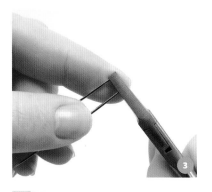

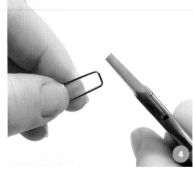

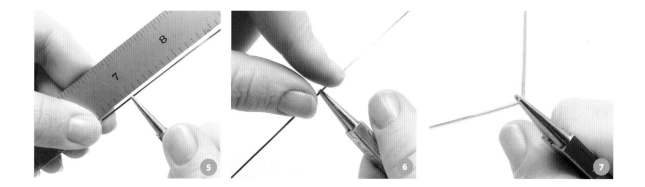

Step 4: Hold the second 14" (35.5 cm) piece of square, gold-filled wire against a ruler and place round-nose pliers at the 7" (18 cm) mark. Use the very tip of the round-nose pliers **(Figure 5)**. Once again, use your thumb and index finger to bend the wire about halfway down **(Figure 6)**.

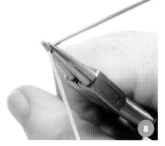

Step 5: **Figure 7** shows the wire bent about halfway. When you have bent the wire as shown, reverse the wire in the pliers and continue bending **(Figures 8 and 9)**.

The taper in the round-nose pliers makes reversing the wire even more important. As you bend the wire, watch the ends to ensure that they are even with each other.

Step 6: Make certain the wire isn't twisted. Use flat-nose pliers to press the wire flat and even **(Figure 10)**. This rounded end will become the clasp end of the bracelet.

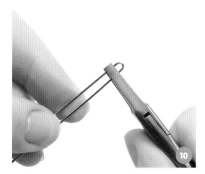

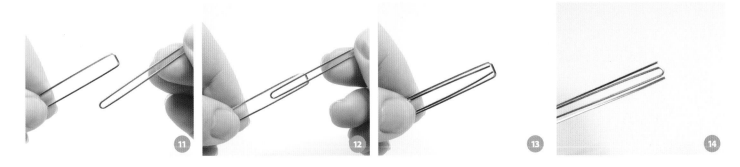

Step 7: Slide the rounded-end wire into the frame wire as shown in **Figures 11 through 14**.

Figure 13 shows how the square end of the frame wire should look. **Figure 14** shows the round end with the frame wires on the outside.

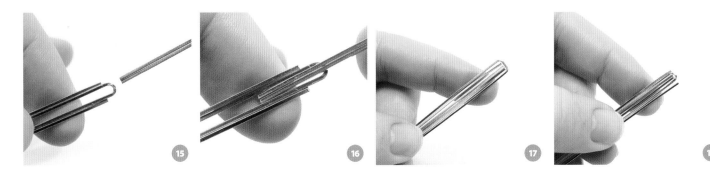

Step 8: Cut two 6¾" (17 cm) pieces of square wire. Keeping the two 6¾" (17 cm) wires even and close together, slide them into the center space **(Figures 15 and 16)**. **Figure 17** shows the two 6¾" (17 cm) wires at the square end. **Figure 18** shows the same wires at the round end.

Step 9: Wrap masking tape about 1" (2.5 cm) from each end and also in the middle of the bracelet **(Figures 19 and 20)**. Wrap the masking tape all the way around the bracelet, being careful not to let the wires bunch up. Make sure all the wires are in the proper order and keep them that way while wrapping.

If the square end of the frame is too wide, leaving a gap between the frame wires and the inner wires, use flat-nose pliers to press the frame closer to the other wires **(Figure 21)**.

Step 10: Cut a 6" (15 cm) piece of the half-round wire. File one end smooth. With the flat (back) side of the wire facing you, place round-nose pliers about ¼" (6 mm) from the end of the wire and bend it toward you **(Figure 22)**.

Step 11: Bend the wire over so that it is to the left of center **(Figure 23)**. This little hook is called a J hook. (**Figure 23** shows the J hook correctly made: bent off-center to the left.)

Good To Know: Half-Round vs Square Wire

It wasn't terribly long ago that wire wrapping was done with square wire. Square wire is very strong, but it isn't very pretty when used for wire wrapping. Half-round wire has replaced square wire for wrapping wire, and while it's not quite as strong, it sure is prettier! To compensate for the loss of strength, always use half-round wire that is at least the same gauge as the square wire, but preferably a gauge larger. So if you're using 20-gauge (0.8 mm) square wire, use 18-gauge (1.0 mm) half-round wire to wrap with.

Wrapping takes lots of practice. There's simply no way around that!

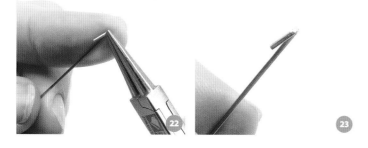

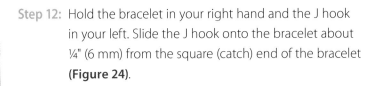

Step 12: Hold the bracelet in your right hand and the J hook in your left. Slide the J hook onto the bracelet about ¼" (6 mm) from the square (catch) end of the bracelet **(Figure 24)**.

Step 13: Now comes the part when you'll wish you had at least eight hands! Use flat-nose pliers to press the J hook closed on the bracelet **(Figure 25)**. The side with the long wire will now be the front of the bracelet.

The wraps on the front of the bracelet should be at perfect right angles to the other wires. On the back side, the end of the J hook should angle toward the square end of the bracelet, as in **Figure 26**. The slant of the wrap wire on the back of the bracelet allows wire from the front to pass around the back side without overlapping.

Step 14: With the flat-nose pliers still holding the wrap, use your index finger to push the wrapping wire over the top of the bracelet and to the back **(Figure 27)**. By using your finger to push the wire over the edge of the bracelet, you should be able to get a good, tight wrap.

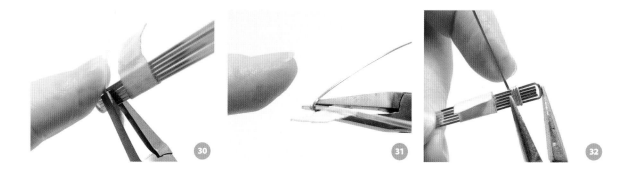

Step 15: **Figure 28** shows the back of the bracelet just before pressing the first wrap into place.

Use flat-nose pliers to press the wire wrap down firmly alongside the J hook **(Figure 29)**. Once again, hold the wrap securely with the flat-nose pliers. Use your index finger to press the wrap wire firmly over to the front of the bracelet **(Figure 30)**.

Step 16: **Figure 31** shows the wrap wire pressed to the front of the bracelet. Use flat-nose pliers to press the wire tightly into place. The wraps should be perfectly straight and should lie right against each other. Continue wrapping until you have three wraps on the front of the bracelet.

Step 17: Check to see if your wraps have shifted position during the wrapping process. If so, use chain-nose pliers to put the wraps back where they're supposed to be **(Figure 32)**.

WHAT IF YOU HAVE A GAP?

The wraps should fit very closely against the bracelet frame, so if they don't, you'll need to do some adjusting. Within the red circle, you can see an unwanted space between the J hook and the wire bundle **(Figure 1)**.

Here you can see that same wrap from the front of the bracelet after more wraps have been made. You'll want to complete a few more wraps to provide an anchor before adjusting the gap. We intentionally made the short end of the J hook longer than it needs to be to make it easier to reopen the wrap and make adjustments **(Figure 2)**.

- Use a penknife to lift up the first wrap **(Figure 3)**.

- Use chain-nose pliers to further unwrap the wire **(Figure 4)**.

- Use chain-nose pliers to squeeze the wrap wire more tightly into place **(Figure 5)**. Grip the very end of the wrap wire with the pliers and pull the wire down and then up, forcing it as close as possible to the bracelet.

Wraps fitting closely against the bracelet frame are shown in **Figure 6**.

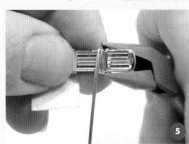

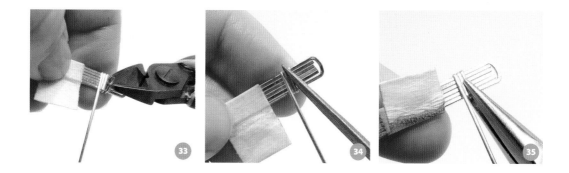

Step 18: Once you are satisfied with all the wraps, cut the wire at the back of the first wrap about ⅛" (3 mm) from the edge of the bracelet **(Figure 33)**.

File the cut end smooth **(Figure 34)**.

Step 19: Now use chain-nose or flat-nose pliers to press the wire back into place **(Figure 35)**.

Figure 36 shows the back of the bracelet with the wraps in place. Always complete the wrap and press it into place, even if you know you'll be lifting it again. This will help the wrap stay in place as you work.

Step 20: Grip the bracelet with flat-nose pliers and lift the last uncut wire with your fingers **(Figure 37)**. Note the proper angle for the wire **(Figure 38)**.

Step 21: Use flush cutters to cut the wrap end ⅛" (3 mm) from the edge of the bracelet **(Figure 39)**. File the cut end smooth and press it firmly into place with pliers. Since we've pressed down this last wrap once before, it will retain its memory of where it's supposed to go as we press it back into place. Note that on the back of the bracelet the wraps are at a slight slant **(Figure 40)**.

Step 22: Repeat the entire wrapping process at the other end of the bracelet, but start the wraps ½" (1.3 cm) from the round (clasp) end **(Figure 41)**. On the back side of the bracelet, all the wraps should slant in the same direction. Begin and end each wrap in exactly the same way.

½" (1.3 cm)

Step 23: Place the bracelet beside a ruler so the middle of the bracelet is between the two wraps you just made—in this case, the 3" mark. With a felt-tipped marker, mark the places where the next wraps will go. Two of the wraps should be about ½" (1.3 cm) from the first two wraps. The other wraps should be about 1" (2.5 cm) apart, making a total of eight wraps **(Figure 42)**. Remove and reapply tape if it's in the way.

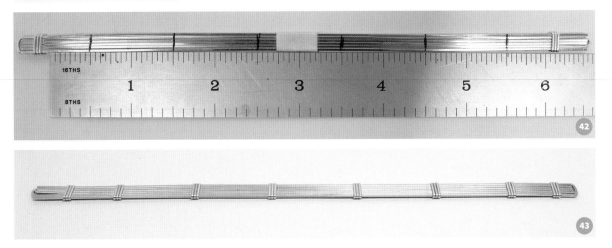

Step 24: **Figure 43** shows the added wraps. The wraps should stay firmly in place. If they don't, try using flat-nose pliers to press them more firmly against the bracelet. Bending the bracelet into a round shape also will help keep the wraps in place. If a wrap remains loose and shifts around, you may have to remove it and re-wrap. After removing the tape, use acetone or Goo-Gone to clean off any residue.

Step 25: Start at one end of the bracelet and use your fingers to bend the wires a little bit at a time. Bend your way to the ends of the bracelet. Keep doing this until the bracelet is round **(Figure 44)**.

Step 26: When the bracelet is smooth and circular, use nylon-jaw pliers to curve the ends into a more oval shape **(Figure 45)**.

Step 27: Using chain-nose pliers, push the square wires at each end of the bracelet to the back side **(Figure 46)**. The square wire is very strong, so bend them one at a time. This will help prevent the wraps from moving as you work.

TIP: What if the bends are too sharp? If you happen to bend the bracelet a bit too much, use nylon-jaw pliers to press the sharp bend into a smoother bend as seen here.

Step 28: Grasp the first wraps with flat-nose pliers to prevent them from moving and use chain-nose pliers to pull each square wire farther to the back side the bracelet **(Figure 47)**. Repeat the same process on the catch end of the bracelet. Make sure that each wire is equally aligned with its neighbors **(Figure 48)**.

Step 29: While holding the wraps with flat-nose pliers, continue bending the end wires inward and down, folding them over the wraps **(Figure 49)**.

Step 30: **Figure 50** shows the square wires folded over the wraps. Use flush cutters to trim the square wires even, leaving enough wire to cover the silver wraps. Use the barrette file to file the cut ends smooth. File in one direction only **(Figure 51)**.

Step 31: Use flat-nose pliers to press the filed square wires into place over the silver wraps **(Figure 52)**. Use chain-nose pliers to press the wire ends inward to ensure that no wire ends are sticking out to irritate the skin **(Figure 53)**.

Figure 54 shows the finished ends. The smooth ends won't irritate the skin, and the curved square wires ensure that no wires will ever pull away from the bracelet.

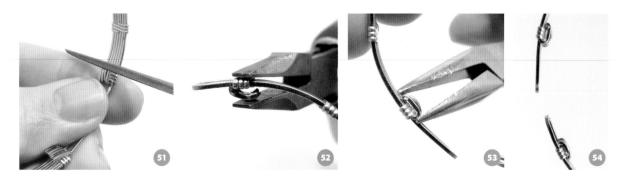

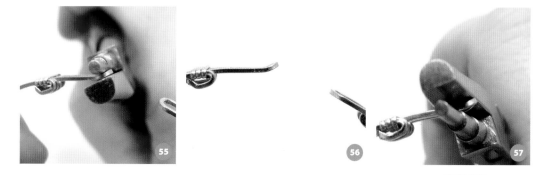

Step 32: Using step-nose pliers, place the clasp on the first, or smallest step. Bend the clasp end up slightly **(Figures 55 and 56)**.

Step 33: Using the step-nose pliers, place the clasp on the second step (near the end of the clasp as shown in **Figure 57**) and roll the pliers so that the clasp forms a U **(Figure 58)**. Note that the little upward curve you just made is flattening out. Not to worry—the curve won't flatten out all the way. This will help the clasp to join the catch more easily.

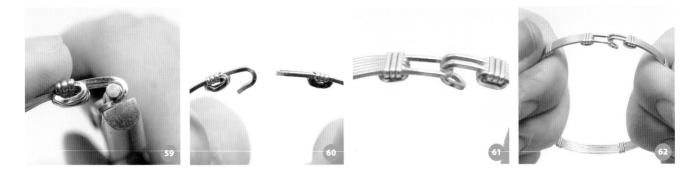

Step 34: Move the clasp to the smallest step of the pliers to complete the curve **(Figure 59)**. To prevent the curve from becoming uneven, curve a little and then move the pliers to the other side and curve a little more. **Figures 60 and 61** show the finished clasp. The clasp should fit easily into the square catch. If it doesn't, use flat-nose pliers to gently narrow the clasp.

Step 35: To finish the bracelet, form it into a comfortable oval shape. Close the bracelet and, using two fingers on each side, gently pull outward to form a graceful oval shape **(Figure 62)**. If the bracelet is too oval, use three fingers on the top and the bottom to shape the bracelet to your liking.

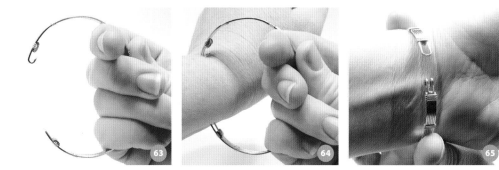

PUTTING ON YOUR BRACELET

Now that your bracelet is finished, here's the proper way to put it on your wrist. The natural tendency is to slide the bracelet over your hand. Don't do that! Over time, the bracelet will get twisted out of shape.

Step 1: Spread the bracelet just enough to be able to slide it on to your wrist from the side **(Figures 63 and 64)**.

Step 2: Turn the bracelet so the clasp is underneath your wrist **(Figure 65)**.

Step 3: Close the clasp and you're done **(Figure 66)**!

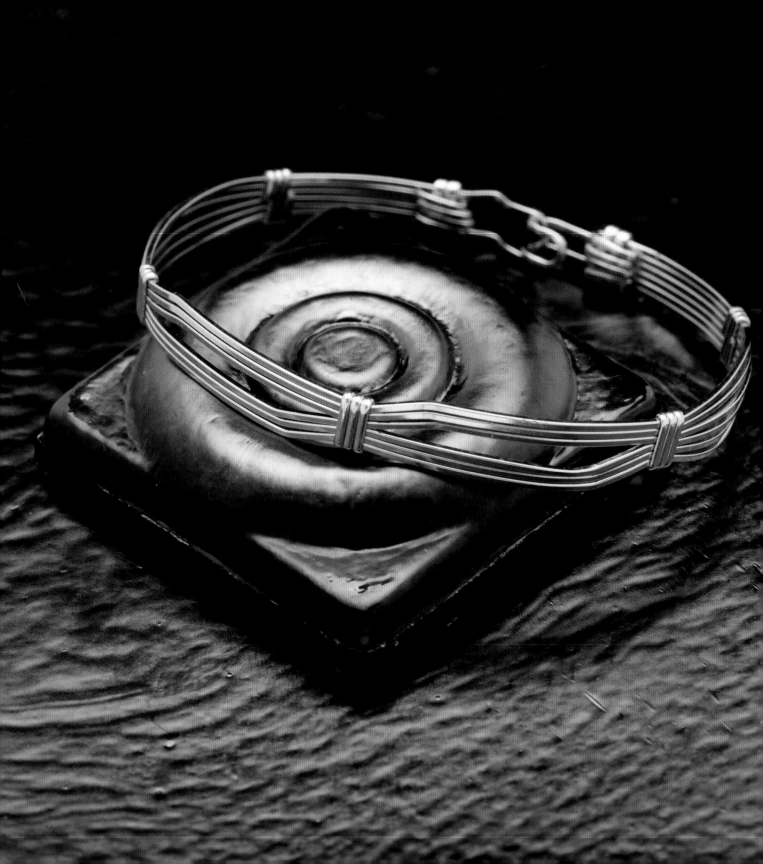

Dress-Up Bracelet

A very simple technique gives the Basic Bracelet a complete makeover. Using just a standard penknife and a little creativity can transform a plain bracelet into an artistic and elegant piece!

TOOLS AND EQUIPMENT
Same as for Basic Bracelet, page 33

YOU'LL NEED
Same as for Basic Bracelet, page 33, except only 30" (76 cm) of half-round wire

TIP: You might have to use flat-nose pliers to hold the wrap wires during the spreading process, especially if you are using sterling silver, which is softer than gold-filled wire.

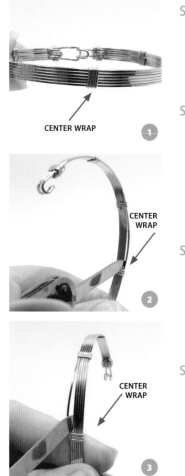

CENTER WRAP ①

Step 1: Follow the instructions on pages 34–46 to make a basic bracelet with the following exception: Arrange the wraps so that one wrap falls in the center of the bracelet **(Figure 1)**. Our example has a total of five wraps.

Step 2: Now start dressing it up by altering the wires on either side of the center wrap. From the back side of the bracelet, insert the blade of a pen knife between the outside wire and the remaining wires, and pull the blade down to the center wrap **(Figure 2).** This will open up a slight space.

CENTER WRAP ②

Step 3: Now bring the blade to the front of the bracelet and rotate the blade counterclockwise, which will angle the wire out **(Figure 3)**. Repeat this on the opposite side of the bracelet, on the other side of the center wrap **(Figure 4)**. Make the bends as symmetrical as possible.

Step 4: Bring the knife blade to the back side of the bracelet and separate the second wires the same way you did the outside wires. Bend the second wires to match the outside wires **(Figure 5)**.

CENTER WRAP ③

CENTER WRAP ④

⑤

⑥

Step 5: Repeat on both sides of the bracelet until you have the "oblique diamond" design shown in **Figure 6**. Because opening the wires makes them shift a little, we'll come back and finish this design later.

Step 6: Move the knife blade to the back side of the wires between the next set of wraps and spread them evenly **(Figure 7).**

Step 7: On the front side, insert the knife blade full length, from wrap to wrap, and spread the wires until you have an even pattern **(Figures 8 through 10)**. After you have spread the wires, move to the opposite section and spread those wires in a similar fashion.

Step 8: Now return to the oblique diamond and finish bending the remaining wires to match the design shown in **Figure 11**. The finished bracelet has three designs: plain, fanned, and oblique diamond **(Figure 12).**

Walk-Along Bracelet

The simple addition of stepped wraps, which we call "walk-along wraps," converts the Basic Bracelet into a sophisticated-looking piece of jewelry. You can use the walk-along wrap to embellish a variety of jewelry, either using just a few wraps, or more than a dozen, as we have in the following project.

TOOLS AND EQUIPMENT

Flush cutters

Nylon-jaw pliers (for straightening wire)

Chain-nose pliers

Flat-nose pliers

Flat file

Ruler

Masking tape

Acetone or Goo-Gone

YOU'LL NEED

About 28" (71 cm) of 20-gauge (0.8 mm) square, half-hard gold-filled wire

About 36" (91 cm) of 18-gauge (1.0 mm) half-round, half-hard sterling silver wire

Step 1: Cut and straighten a 14" (35.5 cm) length of square wire. Using a pair of small flat-nose pliers, make a frame (refer to the Basic Bracelet to review how this is done). For this bracelet, you will need only one frame. The U will be the catch, but we'll make the clasp a different way.

Step 2: Cut and straighten four 6¾" (17 cm) lengths of the same type of wire and tape the wires evenly inside the frame. You will have one frame with four wires inside and six cut wires at the other end.

Step 3: Now, let's make two walk-along wraps at the catch end of the bracelet. Cut and straighten about a 6" (15 cm) length of the half-round wire.

Step 4: Wrap two-and-one-half turns, starting the turns on the back side of the bracelet about ¼" (6 mm) from the inside end of the frame (refer to the Basic Bracelet to review making wraps). As you wrap, press the wire tightly against the frame with chain-nose or flat-nose pliers. **Figure 1** shows the front side of the bracelet with two-and-one-half turns completed (it looks like three turns from the front).

Step 5: Using chain-nose pliers, hold the last turn firmly at the very bottom and bend the wire to the right with your fingers **(Figure 2)**.

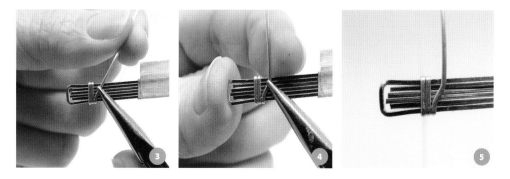

Step 6:   Reposition the pliers **(Figure 3)** and bend the wire straight up **(Figures 4 and 5)**.

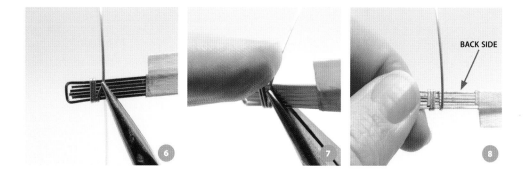

BACK SIDE

Step 7:   Grip the wire firmly with chain-nose pliers **(Figure 6)** and bend it to the back side of the bracelet with your index finger **(Figure 7)**. While bending the wire, press it closely against the frame. This will give you a much tighter wrap that won't move.

Figure 8 shows the back side of the bracelet with the wire pushed as far as possible.

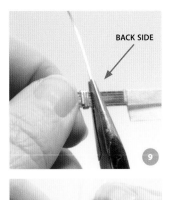

BACK SIDE

9

Step 8: Using chain-nose pliers, press the wire firmly against the back side of the bracelet **(Figure 9)**. Bend the wire slightly to the right, preparing to bring it straight across to the front of the bracelet **(Figure 10)**. The back wires will always be at an angle; the front wires should always be straight.

Step 9: Hold the wire again with chain-nose pliers and push it to the front of the bracelet with your finger, keeping it as straight and snug as possible **(Figure 11)**. Add two more straight wraps, as you normally would **(Figure 12)**.

Step 10: **Figure 13** shows how the back side should look. On the front, hold the wire at the bottom, just as you did before, and start another walk-along wrap **(Figure 14)**.

BACK SIDE

10

BACK SIDE

11

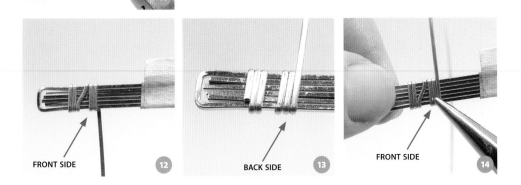

FRONT SIDE **12**

BACK SIDE **13**

FRONT SIDE **14**

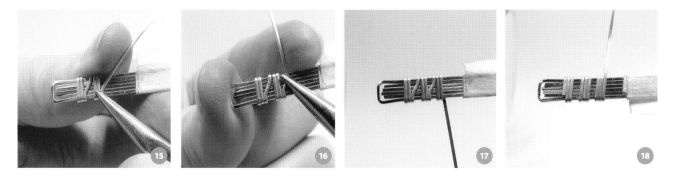

Step 11: Hold the last turn with chain-nose pliers, just as you did before, and bend the wire to the right **(Figure 15)**. Reposition the pliers and bend the wire straight up with your finger **(Figure 16)**.

Step 12: Bring the wire to the back side and press it in place with the chain-nose pliers. Complete two more straight turns across the front of the bracelet **(Figure 17)**. **Figure 18** shows the back side at this point.

Step 13: Cut the wrap wire, file smooth, and press it against the back of the bracelet. Now make two similar walk-along wraps at the clasp end of the bracelet, this time starting the wraps about ⅜" (1 cm) from the wire ends.

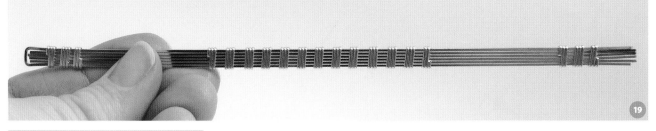

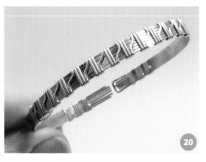

TIP: Now that you know how to make the walk-along wraps, you can spice up your bracelet with as many of them as you want. Twelve walk-alongs have been added to the center of this bracelet. The precise length of wire needed is difficult to calculate, but a rough estimate is that each complete walk-along wrap, which consists of two straight wraps connected by the angled "walk-along," typically requires a little under 6" (15 cm) of wire. The twelve walk-along wraps will need about 24" (61 cm) of wire.

Figure 19 shows the back side of the bracelet. Notice that all wraps on the back side are angled.

Step 14: Clean any tape residue with acetone or Goo-Gone. Using your fingers, bend the bracelet into an oval (**Figures 20 and 21**).

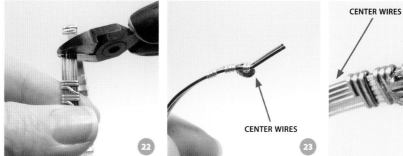

CENTER WIRES

CENTER WIRES

CENTER WIRES

Step 15: Trim all six wires at the clasp end of the bracelet so they extend about ⅜" (1 cm) beyond the wrap **(Figure 22)**. If the wires are a little shorter than ⅜" (1 cm), it's okay.

Step 16: Using chain-nose pliers, bend the center four wires to the back side of the bracelet, leaving the frame wires straight for now **(Figures 23 and 24)**. You can see how to fold the wires under in the Basic Bracelet.

BACK SIDE

Step 17: Grasp one of the frame wires with the smallest step of the step-nose pliers and curl it toward the back side of the bracelet, forming a loop. You may have to reposition the pliers to complete the curl **(Figures 25 and 26)**.

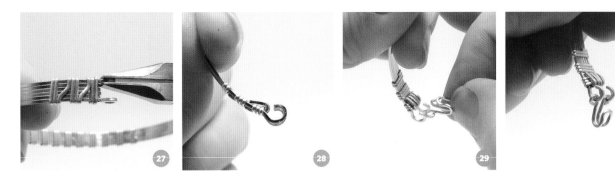

Step 18: Curl the opposite frame wire into a similar loop, then straighten both loops with flat-nose pliers **(Figure 27)**. Reopen the loops just enough to accept the clasp **(Figure 28)**.

Step 19: Make a clasp, as detailed in the Catch and Clasp instructions, and slip it onto the opened loops **(Figures 29 and 30)**. Close the loops with chain-nose pliers **(Figure 31)**. The loops should be big enough to allow the clasp to move freely **(Figure 32)**.

Step 20: Connect the clasp to the catch by gently squeezing the bracelet together **(Figures 33 and 34)**.

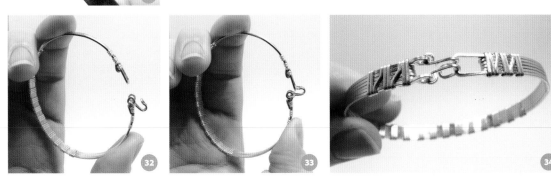

Variation

Add a flourish to that plain old catch by giving it a couple of bends with step-nose pliers.

Make a curve near the wrap by bending either upward or downward with the pliers.

Then bend the clasp again, this time in the opposite direction of the first curve.

Very pretty, don't you think?

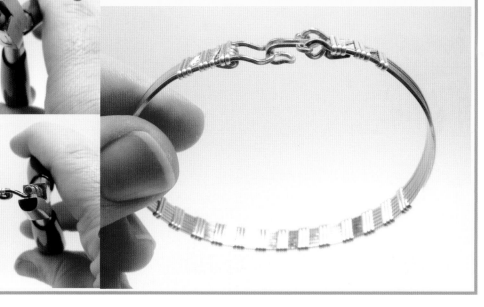

Bow Tie Bracelet

This delicate-looking, yet explosively pretty bracelet is embellished with silver beads. The clasp is made separately and attached to loops at the clasp end. Its outward-radiating lines suggest energy and fun. We hope you will enjoy wearing it as much as you do making it!

TOOLS AND EQUIPMENT

Flush cutters

Nylon-jaw pliers (for straightening wire)

Flat-nose pliers

Round-nose pliers

Chain-nose pliers

Step-nose pliers

Flat file

Penknife

³⁄₁₆" (5 mm) dowel or step mandrel

Ruler

Masking tape

Acetone or Goo-Gone

YOU'LL NEED

About 50" (127 cm) of 21-gauge (0.7 mm) square, half-hard gold-filled wire

About 28" (40.5 cm) of 18-gauge (1.0 mm) half-round, half-hard gold-filled wire

About 1¾" (4.5 cm) of 20-gauge (0.8 mm) square gold-filled wire for clasp

About 1" (3.8 cm) of 16-gauge (1.3 mm) half-round, dead-soft silver wire for catch

28 silver, 3mm beads *Note:* These beads must have a hole big enough for them to slide onto the 21-gauge (0.7 mm) square wire.

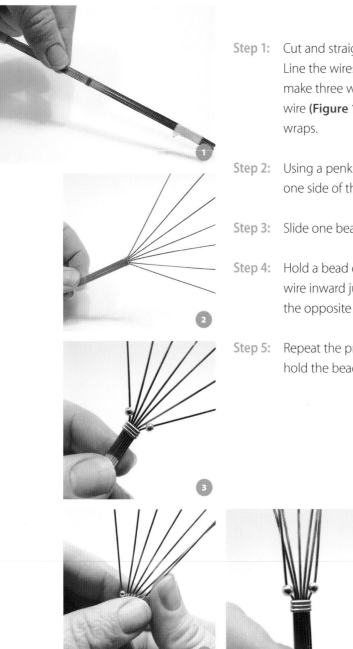

Step 1: Cut and straighten seven pieces of square wire 7" (18 cm) long. Line the wires up evenly, wrap the ends with masking tape, then make three wraps at the center using the 18-gauge half-round wire **(Figure 1)**. See the Basic Bracelet for details on making wraps.

Step 2: Using a penknife or similar tool, spread the wires evenly apart on one side of the center wrap **(Figure 2)**.

Step 3: Slide one bead onto each of the two outer wires **(Figure 3)**.

Step 4: Hold a bead down firmly against the wrap and bend the outside wire inward just enough to keep the bead in place. Repeat on the opposite side **(Figures 4 and 5)**.

Step 5: Repeat the process with the next two wires **(Figure 6)**. Always hold the beads securely while bending the wire.

Step 6: Slide beads onto the third wires, then the center wire; carefully squeeze all the wires together **(Figure 7)**.

Step 7: When the wires are together and the beads are aligned, use flat-nose pliers and your fingers to bring the wires as close together as possible **(Figure 8)**. Use chain-nose pliers to compress the wires close to the bead cluster **(Figure 9)**.

Step 8: Tape the wires together near the ends to help keep them from spreading. Make three wraps of the half-round wire close to the bead cluster **(Figure 10)**. After completing the wraps, remove the tape and spread the wires again to prepare them for more beads and to keep the wraps in place **(Figure 11)**.

Step 9: Continue wrapping and adding beads until you have made four bead clusters, as shown in **Figure 12**. There will be a total of four bead clusters and five sets of wraps.

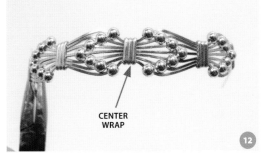

CENTER
WRAP

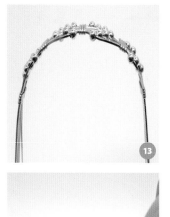

Step 10: Bend the bracelet into a curve as you add bead clusters **(Figure 13)**. As you work, apply some pressure against the back side of the beads to force them to the front side of the bracelet **(Figure 14)**.

Step 11: Cut the five center wires on both ends of the bracelet back ⅝" (1.5 cm), which will leave the two outside wires longer by ⅝" (1.5 cm) **(Figure 15)**.

Step 12: Tape the wires tightly together and make three wraps of half-round wire, starting about ⅛" (3 mm) from the end of the center wires **(Figure 16)**. After completing three wraps, push the wraps to the end of the center wires **(Figure 17)**.

Step 13: Turn the outer wires slightly up to help keep the wraps from slipping off while you form the bracelet curve **(Figure 18)**.

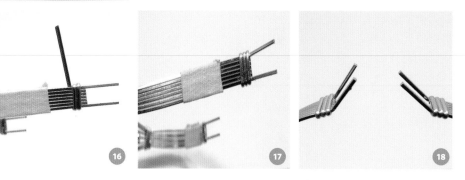

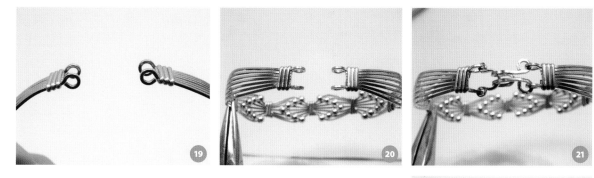

Step 14: Remove any masking tape residue with acetone or Goo-Gone. Bend the bracelet to fit your wrist, then cut the end wires off to a ⅜" (1 cm) length. Using the smallest diameter of step-nose pliers, curl the end wires into loops. Form identical loops on the catch end of the bracelet **(Figure 19)**. To review this process, see the Walk-Along Bracelet.

Step 15: Using a penknife, separate the wires uniformly (see the Dress-Up Bracelet).

Figure 20 shows the bracelet curved into shape, the end wires at the catch and clasp ends looped, and the wires gracefully spread.

Step 16: Make a closure as instructed for the Catch and Clasp. **Figures 21 and 22** show the catch and clasp connected.

Variation

Customizing the Bow Tie Bracelet is easy. In this example, the number and style of wraps have been changed, and a variety of beads and coiled niobium wire are used for the embellishments.

Celtic Knot Bracelet

How did you ever tie that beautiful silver into such a complex knot? That's what they'll ask when you show off this smooth and silky bracelet.

TOOLS AND EQUIPMENT

Flush cutters

Nylon-jaw pliers

Step-nose pliers

Chain-nose pliers

Round-nose pliers

Flat-nose pliers

Flat file

⅜" (1 cm) dowel or step mandrel

Ruler

YOU'LL NEED

About 31" (79 cm) of 14-gauge (1.6 mm) half-round, dead-soft or half-hard sterling silver wire

About 5" (12.5 cm) of 16-gauge (1.3 mm) round, dead-soft silver wire for jump rings

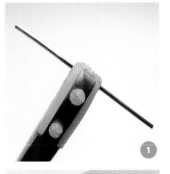

MAKE THE KNOTS

Step 1: Cut and straighten two pieces of half-round wire 2¼" (5.5 cm) long. Hold the wire firmly in the center with nylon-jaw pliers, with the flat part of the wire against one jaw and the round part against the other **(Figure 1)**. With the round side facing you, press toward the pliers with your fingers, starting a bend **(Figure 2)**. You are making a loop by bending the wire on one of its edges, not on either the round or flat side.

Step 2: With the wire on its edge, curve it around a ⅜" (1 cm) diameter dowel or step mandrel **(Figures 3 and 4)**. If the wire twists off its edge, straighten it immediately with nylon-jaw pliers **(Figure 5)**.

Step 3: Continue to bend the wire until a U shape is achieved **(Figure 6)**. Keep the two ends even with each another.

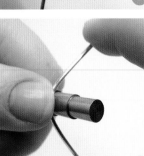

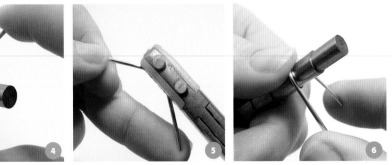

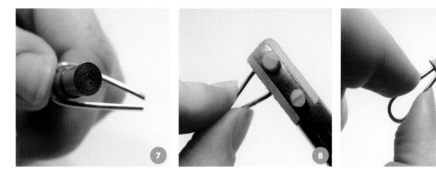

Step 4: Now bring the two ends together **(Figure 7)**. Hold the wire with nylon-jaw pliers and squeeze the two ends even closer **(Figure 8)**. Hold the ends with flat-nose pliers and pinch the legs close together **(Figures 9 through 11)**.

Step 5: With the round side of the wire facing up, curve the U downward **(Figure 12)**.

Now bend the second wire into a U shape and squeeze the legs together, just as you did with the first wire.

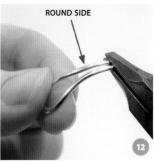

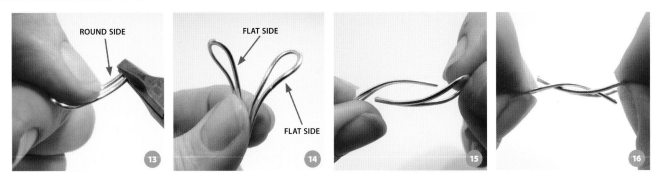

Step 6: With the round side of the second U facing up, bend the U upward (**Figure 13**), making it the opposite of the first U (**Figure 14**).

Step 7: Keeping the round side of the two curved U shapes facing upward, connect them together (**Figures 15 and 16**). This forms a "knot." Pull the pieces, making the knot tighter (**Figures 17 and 18**).

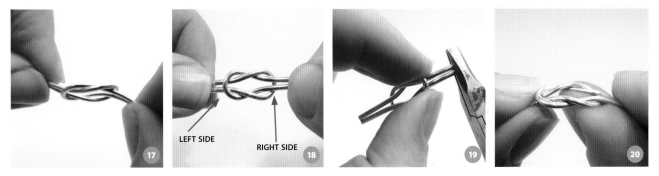

Step 8: Notice that we've identified a right and left side of the knot: On the right side, the end wires travel on top of the other U; on the left side, the end wires travel under the other U.

Trim the end wires to the same length and file smooth (**Figure 19**). The wires should measure about ⅜" (1 cm) from the knot.

Step 9: With the round side of the wires facing upward, curve the piece just a little (**Figure 20**).

Step 10: Using the smallest step of step-nose pliers, curl the end wires on the right side of the knot toward the *flat* side of the wire, forming loops **(Figures 21 through 23)**. Curl only one wire at a time and curl them so they make firm contact with the knot; this will help keep the knot tight.

Step 11: After you have looped the end wires on the right side of the knot, loop the wires on the left side, but curl these wires upward, toward the *round* side of the wire. After the ends are looped, slip the step-nose pliers through both loops to align them **(Figure 24)**.

Step 12: Repeat Steps 1 through 11 for the desired number of knots. Six knots should be adequate for about a 7" (18 cm) bracelet.

RIGHT SIDE OF KNOT

21

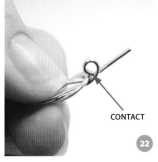

CONTACT

22

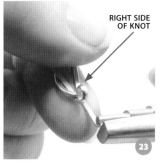

RIGHT SIDE OF KNOT

23

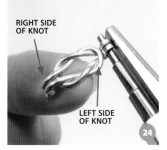

RIGHT SIDE OF KNOT

LEFT SIDE OF KNOT

24

CONNECT THE KNOTS

The knots are connected with jump rings having an inside diameter of about ¼" (6 mm), made of 16-gauge (1.3 mm) round, dead-soft silver wire. If you need to review how to make jump rings, please see Making Jump Rings in the Wire Fundamentals chapter.

Step 1:   Open a jump ring by bending the two ends to the side with chain-nose pliers (never pull them back to widen the gap), then slide it through the loops **(Figure 25)**. Connect the left side of one knot to right side of the next.

Step 2:   Close the jump ring **(Figure 26)**. To review opening and closing jump rings please see Making Jump Rings in the Wire Fundamentals chapter. You now have the first set of connected knots **(Figure 27)**. Continue connecting with jump rings until you have a strand of six knots.

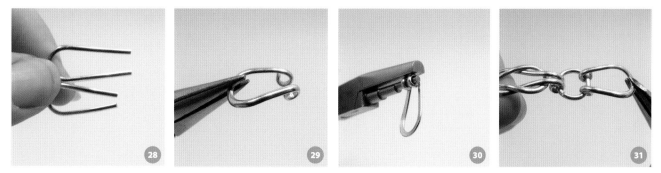

MAKING THE CATCH AND CLASP

Now make a catch and clasp that complement the design of the bracelet.

Step 1: Cut and straighten a piece of the half-round wire 1¾" (4.5 cm) long. Using the same type of wire, cut and straighten a piece 2¼" (5.5 cm) long.

Step 2: Curve both wires on edge around a ⅜" (1 cm) diameter dowel or step mandrel until you have shaped both of them into a U **(Figure 28)**.

Step 3: Using the smallest step of step-nose pliers, form loops on the ends of the smaller U, curling them toward the flat side of the wire **(Figure 29)**. Align by inserting the step-nose pliers through both loops **(Figure 30)**.

Step 4: Connect the catch to the bracelet with a jump ring **(Figure 31)**. The catch should swing freely. If it needs adjustment, try squeezing the loops closer together. If that doesn't do the trick, you may have to remove the catch and widen the loops slightly.

Step 5: Using the smallest step of step-nose pliers, form loops on the ends of the remaining U, curling them toward the flat side of the wire. Align by inserting the step-nose pliers through both loops.

Step 6: With the step-nose pliers inserted through the loops, place round-nose pliers across the U (closer to the U-shaped part than the looped ends), and curl the U **(Figures 32 and 33)**.

Step 7: Using round-nose pliers, continue to curl the broad U-shaped end closer to the loops. Then use the round-nose pliers to nudge the wires near the loops closer together **(Figure 34)**.

Step 8: At this point, you may need to straighten the back side of the clasp **(Figure 35)**. Continue to squeeze the wires closer until you have an even, balanced clasp as shown in **Figure 36**.

Step 9: Attach the clasp to the bracelet with a jump ring, just as you did with the catch. Make sure the clasp has its hook facing up, as shown in **Figure 37**.

TIP: What if the clasp is uneven? Turn the clasp around and place it back onto the step-nose pliers. Keeping the clasp on the step-nose pliers, use the round-nose pliers to adjust the uneven portion.

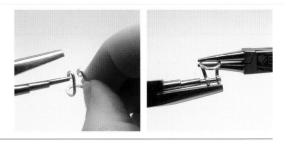

Step 10: You'll have to work with the clasp and catch a little to get them to fit together securely and smoothly. If you need to widen the catch, spread it apart with chain-nose pliers as shown in **Figure 38**. Spread in small increments—you don't want to widen it too much.

Step 11: Adjust the catch and clasp—they must be tilted at an angle to slide together, as shown in **Figure 39**. This will ensure they don't come apart while the bracelet is worn (See finished catch and clasp in **Figures 40 and 41**.)

Variations

Once you have some skill making this bracelet, you can try some relatively exotic variations.

Knots of gold-filled and sterling silver wire; jump rings of gold-filled rose gold.

Simply make knots and add jump rings and ear wires—a perfect match for the Celtic Knot Bracelet!

CHAPTER FOUR

Taking Projects to the Next Level

Ah, the fun stuff! Russ, our guest artist, shows you how to make a very pretty ring. We love this guy and think you will, too! You'll also learn to make some eye-popping bracelets, earrings, and pendants. One of the pendants will teach you how to mount virtually any stone. We've included variations of most of the projects to get your creative juices flowing. Hopefully, you'll see many more possibilities and come up with unique designs that are your very own!

Reef Knot Bracelet

Simpler to make than it looks, this bracelet is also called a Celtic or lover's knot. Its simple elegance can be varied by adding beads to the sides or removing the stone from the center.

TOOLS AND EQUIPMENT

Flush cutters

Step-nose pliers

Flat-nose pliers

Nylon-jaw pliers

Chain-nose pliers

Flat file

Penknife

¼" (6 mm) diameter dowel or stepped mandrel

⅜" (1 cm) diameter dowel or stepped mandrel

⁵⁄₁₆" (8 mm) diameter dowel or stepped mandrel

Ruler

Felt-tipped marker

Masking tape

Acetone or Goo-Gone

YOU'LL NEED

About 44" (112 cm) of 21-gauge (0.7 mm) square, half-hard gold-filled wire

About 20" (51 cm) of 18-gauge (1.0 mm) half-round, half-hard gold-filled or sterling silver wire

About 2¾" (7 cm) of 20-gauge (0.8 mm) square, dead-soft gold-filled wire

6mm faceted stone

6mm gold-filled snap setting

Four or more beads about 3mm in diameter. *Note:* The holes in the beads should be big enough to allow the beads to slide onto 21-gauge (0.7 mm) square wire. It may be necessary to experiment with different bead sizes in order to get a proper fit.

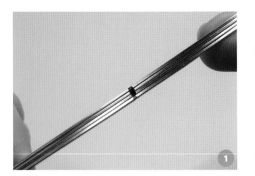

Step 1: Straighten about 36" (91.5 cm) of the 21-gauge (0.71 mm) wire and cut it into four pieces 9" (23 cm) long. Lay the pieces evenly side by side and mark the center of the wires with a felt-tipped marker **(Figure 1)**.

Step 2: Curve two of the wires into a U shape by bending over about a ⅜" (1 cm) diameter dowel or step ring mandrel **(Figure 2)**. Curve the two remaining wires over about a ⁵⁄₁₆" (8 mm) dowel or step mandrel.

Step 3: Fit the U-shaped wires closely inside each other—smaller diameter U inside larger—so you have two pairs, and secure each pair with tape, as shown in **Figure 3**. Bend each pair into a slight curve **(Figure 4)**. Make the pairs and curves as identical as possible.

Step 4: Slip the two pairs of wire inside each other, forming a loose "knot" **(Figure 5)**. Pull the two pairs of wire, tightening the knot to a moderate degree **(Figure 6)**.

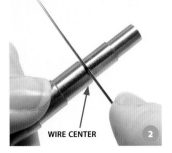

WIRE CENTER

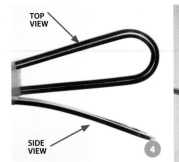

TOP VIEW

SIDE VIEW

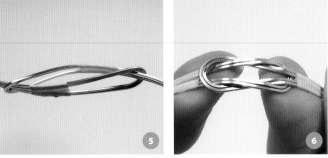

Step 5: Once the knot is tightened, use chain-nose pliers to spread the opening enough to accommodate the snap setting for the 6mm stone, which will be placed in the center **(Figure 7)**.

Step 6: Press the snap setting firmly over the back side of the stone **(Figures 8 and 9)**. This may require some force before the setting snaps into place.

Step 7: To help hold the stone in the setting, use chain-nose pliers to lightly squeeze all the prongs side by side, as shown in **Figure 10**. Squeeze the prongs on one side, then go to the opposite side and do the same, continuing until all the prongs are snug and even. The idea is to squeeze the prongs just enough to tighten the stone a little.

Step 8: Straighten and cut a 7" (8 cm) length of the 21-gauge (0.7 mm) wire. This wire will hold the stone and beads. Slide one end of this wire in the center, underneath the top end of the knot, as shown in **Figure 11**. Slide the wire down until it is even with the other wires. You may have to remove the tape to accomplish this, but then re-tape after inserting the wire.

WIRE UNDER HERE

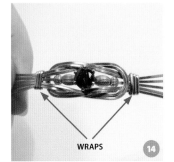

WRAPS

Step 9: Slide on the beads and stone. They should just nestle inside the knot—not too loose, not too tight **(Figure 12)**.

Step 10: Lay the free end of the wire over the knot, align it with the remaining wires, and wrap tape around the wires to hold it in place **(Figure 13)**.

Step 11: Wrap each end of the knots with three turns of the 18-gauge (1.0 mm) half-round wire **(Figure 14)**. You can review the wrapping technique in the Basic Bracelet instructions.

Step 12: Make similar wraps about halfway between the knot and the ends of bracelet **(Figure 15)**. Curve the piece into a bracelet shape, checking its size against your wrist. (This photo also shows the wires spread apart, which we'll explain in Step 15.)

Step 13: Trim all five end wires evenly and then trim the three center end wires back ¼" (6 mm). Wrap the ends with three turns of the 18-gauge (1.0 mm) half-round wire, just as you did above (see **Figure 16**).

Step 14: File the ends of the two outside wires smooth and curl them into loops for the catch and clasp. If you need to review this process, please see the Walk-Along Bracelet.

Step 15: Using a penknife or similar tool, gently bend the wires outward into a pleasing pattern as shown in **Figure 15**. The Dress-Up Bracelet shows this process.

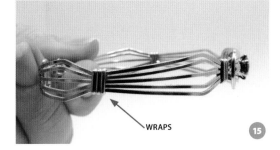

Step 16: Make the catch and clasp from the 20-gauge (0.80 mm) square wire and attach to the bracelet **(Figure 16)**. Please see the Walk-Along Bracelet to review this process. *Note:* Since there are only five wires, the bracelet is fairly narrow, so it will be necessary to bend out the bracelet's attachment loops for an accurate fit.

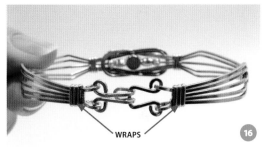

Variation

Here is a Reef Knot Bracelet with added beads and a variation on the wraps and wire shaping.

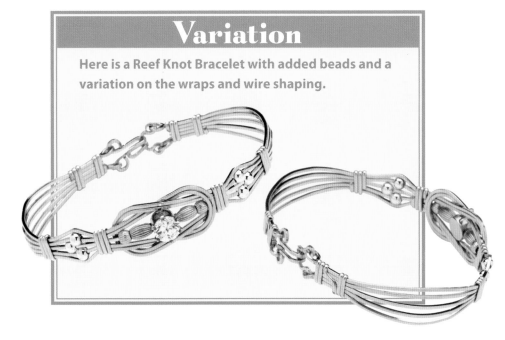

Wire-Wrapped Ring

Here's a pretty little ring that you'll enjoy making and then wearing or giving to someone special. You can vary the look from dainty to dramatic by changing the size of the snap setting and the stone.

This ring and the accompanying instructions were contributed by Russ Sperring. See his biography on page 124. These instructions are for a size 6½ ring.

TOOLS AND EQUIPMENT

Flush cutters

Nylon-jaw pliers (for straightening wire)

Flat-nose pliers

Chain-nose pliers

Flat file

Pin vise

Ring mandrel

Rawhide mallet

Ruler

Felt-tipped marker

YOU'LL NEED

10" (25.5 cm) of 20-gauge (0.8 mm) square, half-hard sterling silver wire

2" (5 cm) of 22-gauge (0.65 mm) half-round, half-hard sterling silver wire

6mm round, sterling silver snap setting

6mm round faceted stone

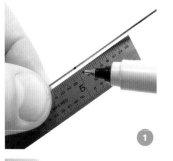

Step 1: Cut and straighten a 10" (25.5 cm) length of the square wire. Mark the center **(Figure 1)**. Use flat-nose pliers to make a slight bend about ⅛" (3 mm) to one side of the center mark **(Figure 2)**.

Step 2: Snap the stone into the setting and slide it onto the wire to the mid-point **(Figure 3)**. See the Reef Knot Bracelet for instructions on setting the stone.

Step 3: With the stone in the center, bend down both sides of the wire **(Figure 4)**.

Place the piece on the ring mandrel at the desired size. Make sure the wire stays flat against the mandrel **(Figure 5)**.

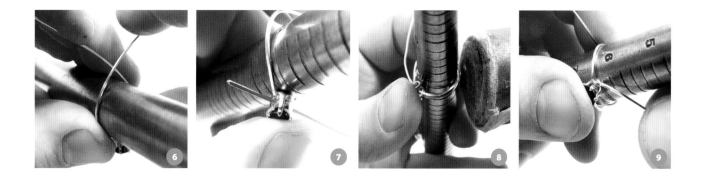

Step 4: In **Figure 6**, notice that the left wire is crossed over the right wire.

Feed the right wire through the setting, as shown in **Figure 7**. Pull the wire tight. From time to time, you may have to use a rawhide mallet to keep the ring's shape. Do this by gently tapping the wire around the mandrel **(Figure 8)**.

Step 5: Bend the wire to the right **(Figure 9)**. Carefully remove the ring from the mandrel, turn it around, and slip it back on **(Figure 10)**.

Step 6: Repeat steps illustrated in **Figures 7 through 9**, feeding the free wire through the setting, pulling tight, and bending it to the right. The ring should now resemble **Figure 11**.

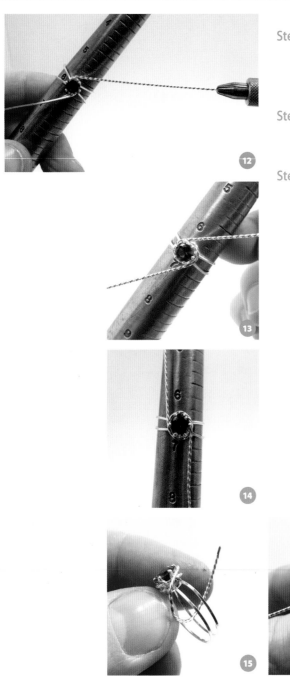

Step 7: Using a pin vise, twist each wire about six turns **(Figure 12)**. Be careful not to over-twist, or you'll break the wire.

Step 8: Now wrap the wires around the setting almost one full clockwise turn **(Figures 13 and 14)**.

Step 9: Remove the ring. Bend one of the wires down and loop it through the inside of the ring **(Figure 15)**. Tighten the wire, bending it up against the setting **(Figure 16)**. Press the wire in place with chain-nose pliers **(Figure 17)**.

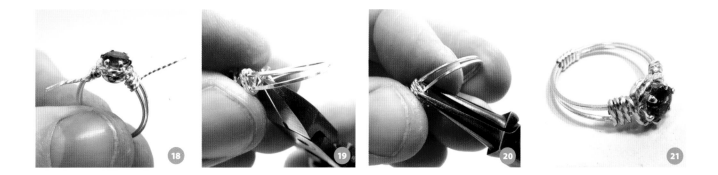

Step 10: Make a total of three wraps around the ring, pressing the wire in place each time you complete a turn, and repeat on the opposite side **(Figure 18)**.

Step 11: Bend the wires in toward the center of the ring and cut them so the ends will fall between the shank wires **(Figure 19)**. File the wire ends smooth and press the wires down so they cannot be felt when the ring is on your finger **(Figure 20)**. Check the ring size by slipping it back onto the mandrel.

Step 12: Cut and straighten 2" (5 cm) of 22-gauge (0.65 mm) half-round wire and wrap the shank wires at the middle back of the ring. This wire will be long enough for five or six turns. Keep the wraps centered by starting your wrapping at the center of the wrap wire and wrapping one side and then the other, moving outward away from the center. **Figure 21** shows the finished ring.

Gem Stone Bracelet

Making this pretty bracelet will give you the skills to create your own unique designs. We've included some variations to help you see some of the many possibilities for modifying this bracelet.

TIP: This bracelet requires two 6½" (16.5 cm) lengths of twisted 22-gauge (0.65 mm) sterling silver round wire. The twisted wire will have a delicate appearance, but will actually be four- or five-thousandths of an inch larger than single 20-gauge (0.8 mm) square wire.

TOOLS AND EQUIPMENT

Flush cutters

Nylon-jaw pliers (for straightening wire)

Step-nose pliers

Flat file

Small, variable-speed electric drill or pin vise

Ruler

Felt-tipped marker

Masking tape

Acetone or Goo-Gone

YOU'LL NEED

About 30" (76 cm) of 20-gauge (0.8 mm) square, half-hard gold-filled wire

About 26" (66 cm) of 22-gauge (0.65 mm) round, dead soft sterling silver wire

About 23" (58.5 cm) of 18-gauge (1.0 mm) half-round, half-hard gold-filled wire

Faceted 6mm stone

6mm gold-filled snap setting

Two 1.2" (1.3 cm) coiled niobium wire "beads"

Step 1: Straighten and cut two 13" (33 cm) lengths of 22-gauge (0.65 mm) round sterling silver wire. Fold each of the wires exactly in half **(Figures 1 and 2)**. Tape the free ends of one of the folded wires with masking tape, rolling the tape smoothly around the wire three or four times **(Figures 3 and 4)**.

Step 2: Place the taped end of the wire in the chuck of a small electric drill or pin vise and tighten securely **(Figure 5)**.

Step 3: Insert the smallest step of a pair of step-nose pliers through the loop on the opposite end of the wire **(Figure 6)**. Step-nose pliers grasp the wire more evenly than round-nose pliers and will have less tendency to break the wire.

TWISTED WIRES

SQUARE WIRES

¼" (6 мм)

Step 4: Hold the pliers in one hand and the drill in the other **(Figure 7)**. Keeping a firm grip on the pliers, turn on the drill and slowly turn the wire into a very tight twist **(Figure 8)**. If the wire pulls out of the chuck, just put it back in and continue. If you're using a pin vise, roll the vise along your thigh to twist the wire.

Step 5: Tape and twist the second wire in the same fashion and try to make the twists as identical as possible to the first twisted wire (**Figure 8** shows a nice, tight twist.)

Step 6: Make a frame from a 15" (38 cm) length of the 20-gauge (0.8 mm) square wire. See Basic Bracelet for details on making the frame. The outside width of the frame should be about ¼" (6 mm). Inside the frame, place the two twisted wires and two 6½" (16.5 cm) lengths of the 20-gauge (0.8 mm) square wire, as shown in **Figure 9**. Tape the wires ¼" (6 mm) from the inside end of the frame. The open space will become the catch.

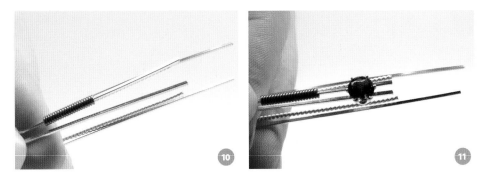

Step 7: Hold up the two square wires and add a ½" (1.3 cm) length of coiled niobium wire to one of the square wires, then slide a faceted 6mm snap set onto both square wires (**Figures 10 and 11**). See the Reef Knot Bracelet for details on snap-setting a stone. If you can't find coiled niobium in the correct length, you can substitute a combination of beads or other embellishments about ³⁄₃₂" (2.4 mm) in width.

Step 8: Slide another coiled niobium wire of the same length onto the square wire but opposite the first coil. Slide the stone and coiled niobium wire to the center of the bracelet. The stone should be 3¼" (8.5 cm) from each end (**Figure 12**).

Step 9: Tape one end next to the embellishments, as shown in **Figure 13**. Curve the bracelet slightly; this will help hold the embellishments in place during the next step **(Figure 14)**.

Step 10: Make four wraps of the 18-gauge (1.0 mm) half-round wire next to the un-taped embellishments, then remove the tape and make four wraps next to the embellishments on the other side **(Figures 15 and 16)**. Bend the wires outward a little to keep the wraps from sliding as you work **(Figure 17)**.

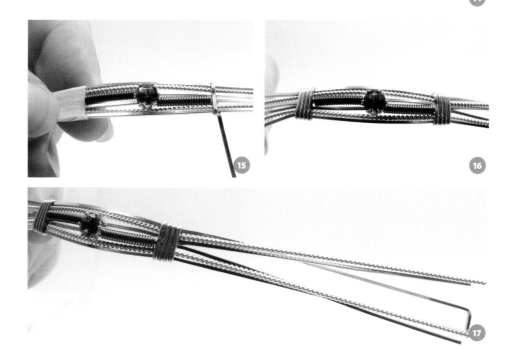

Step 11: Add flair by spreading the wires into artistic patterns and by adding walk-along wraps, as shown in **Figures 18 and 19**. These wraps are described in the Walk-Along Bracelet instructions and spreading wires is covered with the Dress-Up Bracelet. The walk-along wraps should be positioned about halfway between the embellishments and the ends of the bracelet.

Step 12: Finish the bracelet off with more walk-along wraps at the ends and with a clasp made of 20-gauge (0.8 mm) square gold-filled wire **(Figure 20)**. Making the Catch and Clasp is covered in Wire Fundamentals. Remove any masking tape residue with acetone or Goo-Gone.

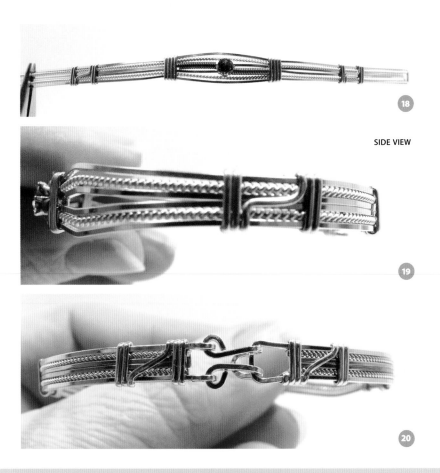

18

SIDE VIEW

19

20

Variations

A more advanced design is shown here. More snap sets have been added, the beads are different, and the wraps are a bit more complex. Otherwise, it's the same bracelet as the one just presented. Note the way the wraps are made on either side of the embellishments. Wrapping this way adds strength to the bracelet.

Here's yet another version; a bracelet sparkling with beads added beyond the center embellishments. The frame is the same as the previous bracelet, except that in this case, the twisted wire is purchased pre-twisted and is made of 20-gauge (0.8 mm) sterling silver.

A fifth wire, a 6 ½" (16.5 cm) length of 20- or 21-gauge (0.8 mm or 0.7 mm) round, half-hard gold-filled wire is added through the middle of the bracelet. This makes adding beads beyond the center easier and also allows the use of beads with a smaller diameter hole.

Here's one more bracelet that's a bit different. This relatively simple design uses 20-gauge (0.8 mm) square, half-hard gold-filled wire for both the frame and the two inside wires. A combination of coiled niobium wire beads and gold-filled beads occupies the space between the wraps, which are made of 18-gauge (1 mm) half-hard, half-round gold-filled wire.

Stone Pendant

Here's a beautiful Spiderweb Imperial Jasper stone framed in gold. The instructions are general, since, sadly, you most likely will not be able to find this exact stone. But, when you do find a beautiful stone, you'll have the skills to make a gorgeous pendant!

TOOLS AND EQUIPMENT

Flush cutters

Nylon-jaw pliers (for straightening wire)

Flat-nose pliers (two pairs)

Step-nose pliers

Round-nose pliers

Chain-nose pliers

Penknife

Ring mandrel

Ruler

Felt-tipped marker

Masking tape

Acetone or Goo-Gone

Sheet of rigid paper or card stock

YOU'LL NEED

21-gauge (0.7 mm) square, half-hard gold-filled wire

18-gauge (1.0 mm) half-round, half-hard gold-filled wire

20-gauge (0.8 mm) half-round, half-hard gold-filled wire

21-gauge (0.7 mm) half-round, half-hard gold-filled wire

Our stone measures about ¾" (2 cm) × 1½" (3.8 cm) × ⅛" (3 mm) thick

Note: Legths of wire will depend on the size of your stone.

Good To Know:

Wrapping stones can be a tricky process, depending upon the size and shape of the stone you choose. Our Spiderweb Imperial Jasper stone is designer cut with a slightly tapered wall, making it a nice piece to wrap.

Step 1: You'll need to find the distance around the stone to know the length of wire to cut for the mounting and bail. Wrap masking tape around the edge. Mark the tape as you start to wrap (**Figure 1**), and when your tape comes around and covers the mark, make another mark on top of the first one (**Figure 2**).

Step 2: Measure the distance between the marks, which in this case is 4" (10 cm), as shown in **Figure 3**. We need an extra 3" (7.5 cm) for the bail, which gives us 7" (18 cm) total wire length.

Step 3: Now we need to decide how many wires to cut. We want to combine enough wires to cover the wall, plus one extra wire. Holding wires up against the edge of the stone, we can see that six will be required (**Figure 4**).

Step 4: For this stone, we will cut and straighten the six 21-gauge (0.7 mm) square wires 7" (18 cm) in length. Line the wires up precisely and mark the center (**Figure 5**). The center is where the first wrap will go.

Step 5: Place the stone on a sheet of rigid paper or card stock and trace around it. Mark points where you want the wraps to be placed (**Figure 6**).

Step 6: Wrap the wires at intervals with masking tape. Using a dowel or ring mandrel the same approximate diameter as the stone's rounded bottom, center the wires and curve them to closely match the stone (**Figure 7**).

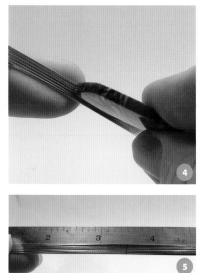

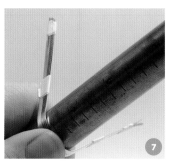

Step 7: To hold the stone in place while fitting the wires, fold a piece of masking tape over itself and stick the stone to a rigid, light-weight surface **(Figure 8)**. Curve and bend the wires to conform to the stone's shape **(Figure 9)**.

Step 8: Now make a wrap at center bottom. Cut and straighten about a 3" (7.5 cm) length of the 21-gauge (0.7 mm) half-round wire. Because it's difficult to know exactly where to start the wrap in order to have it located perfectly in the bottom center of the wires, make a very, very long J hook instead of the usual short one **(Figure 10)**. This allows you to easily add more turns on either side of the wrap to keep it centered. Refer to the Basic Bracelet for details on wrapping.

Step 9: **Figure 11** shows a seven-turn wrap (you can have more turns, if you want) completed and nicely centered. Check the fit again and make any necessary adjustments.

Step 10: Place the wires on the tracing and mark where the next wraps will be placed **(Figure 12)**. You may need to remove the masking tape to make room for the wraps.

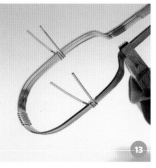

Step 11: Again starting with a long J hook, wrap each location with the 21-gauge (0.7 mm) half-round wire. Make only three turns, leaving extra wire, as shown in **Figure 13**. This way, you can add or subtract a turn if you need to even the wraps up later. Keeping the wraps aligned is a potential problem, as the wires tend to shift as you work with the piece.

Step 12: Using flat-nose pliers and the mandrel, form the top of the piece to fit the stone **(Figure 14)**. If the fit is off too much, you'll have to straighten the wires and try again.

Step 13: After you're pleased with the shape of the wires, secure the neck of the piece with three or four temporary turns of the 20-gauge (0.8 mm) half-round wire **(Figure 15)**.

Step 14: **Figure 16** shows more adjustment being made with flat-nose pliers, squeezing the wires (carefully!) into closer contact with the stone. Now you can finish up the wraps on the sides of the stone. Place a ruler across the wraps to make sure they're even **(Figure 17)**.

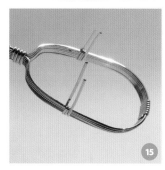

TIP: Why use a temporary wire wrap? These wires will be removed later and replaced with a more complex wrap. Wire is used instead of tape to secure the top because tape will allow the piece to shift too much during the following steps.

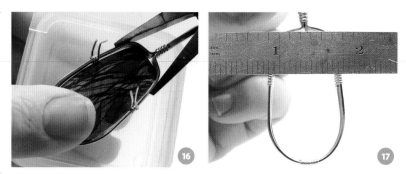

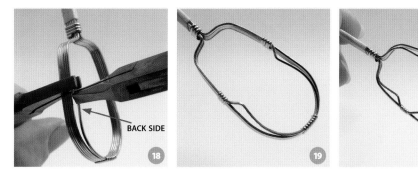

BACK SIDE

Step 15: After the wraps are completed, create four wire supports for the stone, starting with the back side of the piece. Holding the wires securely with flat-nose pliers, use another pair of flat-nose pliers to bend a wire out. Do this by grasping the first wire below a side wrap and rotating the pliers toward the middle of the piece **(Figure 18)**. Repeat this process on the opposite side of the piece **(Figure 19)**, then repeat above the wraps. **Figure 20** shows completed supports on the back side.

Step 16: The stone should fit snugly inside the piece and be evenly supported **(Figure 21)**. Create supports for the stone on the front side the same way you did for the back side, but temporarily leave them shaped as shown in **Figure 22**. Both front and back support wires will be adjusted into their final shape later.

Step 17: Remove the temporary wrap wires or loosen them and push them up the neck to help secure the piece while adding the new wrap wires.

Step 18: From about a 5" (12.5 cm) length of 18-gauge (1.0 mm) half-round wire, make two tight wraps starting about ¼" (6 mm) up the neck from the pendant **(Figure 23)**. The wraps should be made toward the stone. The excess wire will be used later.

BACK SIDE

Step 19: Working from the back side, bend out four of the first wires rising just above the wraps **(Figure 24).** Use the largest step of the step-nose pliers to curl the four wires downward **(Figures 25 and 26)**.

Step 20: After the wires are arranged, make two tight wraps around them with the wires from the previous wraps around the neck **(Figure 27)**.

Step 21: Use a penknife to pry apart the wire ends so they can be curled upward **(Figure 28)**. Use round-nose pliers to curl the four wires upward, one at a time **(Figure 29)**. Use a light touch with the pliers or they'll make ugly indentations in the wire. If any of the wires are too long, cut them off and keep curling them tightly. Hide the wire ends by tucking them into the curl **(Figure 30)**.

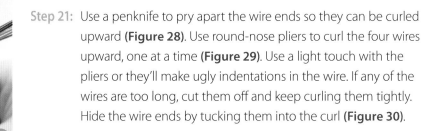

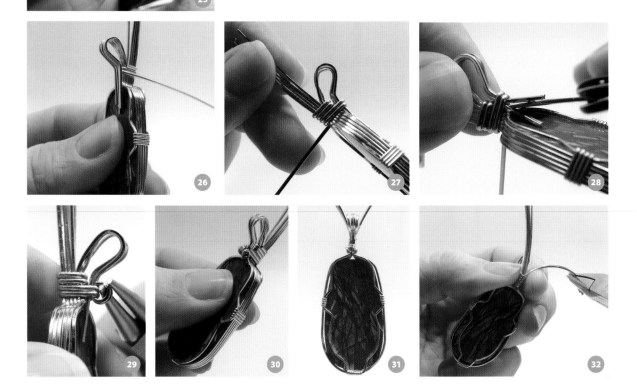

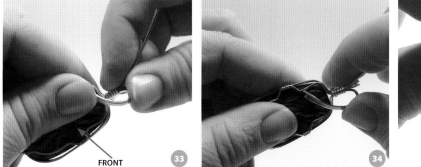

FRONT 33

34

35

Step 22: Using flat-nose pliers or your fingers, split the eight remaining wires apart, four on one side and four on the other, and bend them downward **(Figures 31 and 32)**. These wires should curve smoothly and stay together. Support the wrap with your fingers as you pull, so you don't move the neck out of alignment. Bend the front and back supports into a symmetrical shape, as shown in **Figures 31 and 32**.

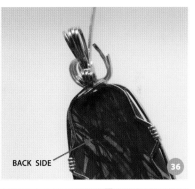

BACK SIDE 36

Step 23: Still supporting the wrap and free wires, bend the four wires smoothly to the front of the pendant and upward **(Figures 33 through 35)**. The wires will want to spring back, but as you tighten the bend, they will stay in place. It's important to bend all four wires at the same time, keeping the square sides together. If you bend them one at a time, they'll never stay in alignment.

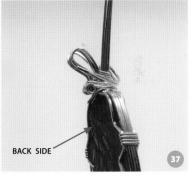

BACK SIDE 37

Step 24: Bend the two bottom wires downward on the back side **(Figures 36 and 37)**.

Return to the front side and adjust the wires to a more pleasing shape, if necessary **(Figure 38)**.

38

Step 25: On the back side, hide the ends of the wires by curling them under so they rest against the bail and the stone **(Figure 39)**. If any of the wires are too long, trim them as needed. Return to the front again and check that the wires are firmly in place **(Figure 40)**.

Step 26: Now, pull two of the remaining four wires down, around, and across the back side, as shown in **Figures 41 and 42**.

Step 27: Bend the two wires tightly around to the front of the pendant and curl them so the ends are tucked into the small space at the top of the bail **(Figure 43)**. You may need to shorten the wires, so trim them as needed.

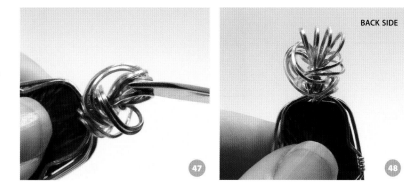

BACK SIDE

47

48

49

Step 28: Using chain-nose pliers, tighten and adjust the two wires (**Figure 44**). Push them deeply into the opening below the wraps.

Step 29: Curve the remaining two wires around to the back, then pull them toward the left side of the bail and curl the ends down tightly against the bottom of the wrap (**Figures 45 and 46**).

You may be thinking, "Man, this thing is ugly!" Don't despair; the next simple steps will finish the transformation of stone and wire into a thing of beauty.

Step 30: Using a penknife, spread the bail wires into graceful shapes (**Figure 47**). When you're finished, you should have a bail resembling the one in **Figures 48 and 49**.

Variation

Here is another pendant using the same techniques. It features gold-filled square and twisted wires.

Patterned Wire Bracelet, Earrings, and Pendant

Never has anything looked so elegant and been so easy to make! This glamorous trio of bracelet, earrings, and pendant definitely calls for a night on the town.

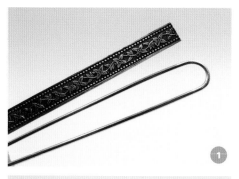

MAKE THE BRACELET

Step 1: Cut a 6" (15 cm) length of patterned wire. If the wire is curved or bent, gently straighten it with your fingers and nylon-jaw pliers.

Step 2: Cut and straighten a 15" (38 cm) length of the 14-gauge (1.6 mm) wire. Curve the wire into a perfect U shape, with the flat side of the wire on the back side of the U **(Figure 1)**. Refer to the Celtic Knot Bracelet to see how this is done. Use a dowel about ⁵⁄₁₆" (8 mm) in diameter to help form the curve.

Step 3: The patterned wire should fit closely inside the frame **(Figure 2)**. Square off and straighten the end of the U with flat-nose pliers. This end will become the bracelet catch **(Figures 3 through 6)**.

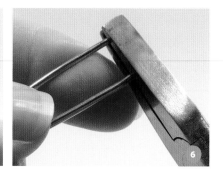

½" (1.3 cm)

Step 4: Tape the frame and patterned wire together, leaving a ½" (1.3 cm) space between the catch end and the patterned wire (**Figure 7**).

TIP: For this project, we've used the walk-along style wrap on the back side of the bracelet, which gives it more strength and rigidity. The wraps can be made from several lengths of wire or from one long piece. The total length of wire required will be about 12" (30.5 cm), but it's best to start with a longer piece, especially if you plan on making the wraps from a single length. We added coiled niobium wire to four of the wraps on this bracelet for that little extra something.

Good To Know:
Choosing Patterned Wire

Even though patterned wire is wider and flatter than what we think of when we hear the word "wire," it's still called patterned wire. That doesn't make much sense, but that's what it's called!

Patterned wire is sold by a number of jewelry supply companies (see Resources) and varies in terms of pattern, width, thickness, and hardness. A lot of patterned wire, such as the examples shown here, is antiqued, which adds depth and dimension to its appearance. Typically, patterned wire is dead soft.

We recommend a thickness of around 0.030" (0.8 mm), about the same as 21-gauge (0.7 mm) wire. Patterned wire much thicker than this can be difficult to form into a bracelet shape, and thinner wire can be too flimsy for a bracelet. Some patterned wire has a beveled, sharp edge, which must be filed flat and smooth.

Step 5: With the 18-gauge (1.0 mm) wire, wrap the square end of the bracelet first. Measure and mark the center of the bracelet, and add wraps at about ½" (1.3 cm) intervals (**Figures 8 and 9**). End the wrapping at the catch end by making three wraps.

After completing all of the wraps, use your fingers to form the bracelet into an oval shape. Use acetone or Goo-Gone to clean off any masking tape residue.

Step 6: Measuring from the wrap, cut the end wires to about ⅜" (1 cm) in length, and roll them into loops using the smallest step on the step-nose pliers.

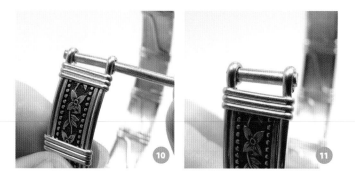

Step 7: Insert the 1" (2.5 cm) piece of 10-gauge (2.6 mm) wire (**Figure 10**) and trim the wire with flush cutters so that just a tiny amount of wire protrudes from each loop (**Figure 11**).

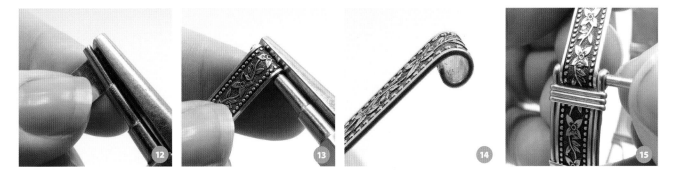

Step 8: Cut a piece of patterned wire 1½" (3.8 cm) in length and file one end smooth. Using the smallest step of the step-nose pliers, roll the smoothed end of the wire into a loop.

To make the loop even, reverse the wire in the pliers several times **(Figures 12 through 14)**.

Step 9: Attach the clasp as shown in **Figure 15**, using the 10-gauge (2.6 mm) wire as a pin. The pin should fit snugly through the clasp and loops but should allow the clasp to move easily.

Step 10: Remove the patterned wire from the bracelet and cut it ½" (1.3 cm) from the loop **(Figure 16)**. Check the fit of the clasp in the catch and file the clasp sides and corners with the smooth file, tapering them as needed **(Figures 17 and 18)**. You only need to file a short distance back from the tip of the clasp.

Step 11: Using the smallest step of the step-nose pliers, curl the clasp end (**Figure 19**). Move the pliers back and forth, curling from one side of the clasp, then the other, to keep them even.

Step 12: File the end as needed for a smooth fit, then curl an additional amount until it resembles **Figures 20 and 21**.

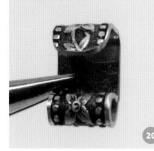

Step 13: Attach the clasp with the pin, then close the bracelet (**Figure 22**). Next, you'll need to tighten the loops, which may need to be cut and shortened. Cut only tiny amounts of the loops at a time, until they can be tightened enough around the pin that it can't fall out (**Figure 23**).

Step 14: To make absolutely certain the pin can't fall out, we'll make a cold connection. Place the bracelet on a strong, rigid surface, with a thin steel plate underneath the pin, as shown in **Figure 24**.

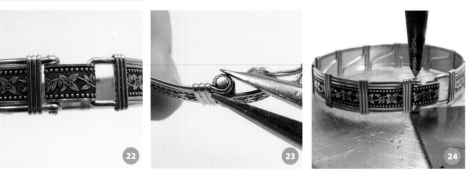

Step 15: Place a center punch in the center of the pin and tap lightly with a steel hammer. Be sure to tap lightly, or your pin will bend. Repeat this on the opposite side. The tapping should cause the pin to flare out at the ends, permanently securing the clasp.

Step 16: To check that the pin can't fall out, try pushing it from each end with the center punch **(Figure 25)**.

MAKE THE EARRINGS

Step 1: Cut two pieces of patterned wire ¾" (2 cm) long and cut and curve two 3" (7.5 cm) pieces of 14-gauge (1.6 mm) wire **(Figure 1)**. You can leave the curves rounded—no need to square them off as you did for the bracelet.

Step 2: Tape the patterned wire over the U-shaped frame, flip the piece upside down, and trace the curve on the patterned wire with a sharp scribe **(Figures 2 through 4)**.

Step 3: Using flush cutters, trim along the scribed line, then file smooth **(Figure 5)**. Repeat this for the remaining piece, then tape the pieces inside their frames **(Figure 6)**.

7

8

9

10

Step 4: Cut and straighten a 6" (15 cm) length of the 18-gauge (1.0 mm) wire. Starting on the back side of the patterned wire, make three wraps with the 18-gauge (1.0 mm) wire **(Figure 7)**. Flare the wire ends outward slightly to prevent the wraps from slipping off **(Figure 8)**.

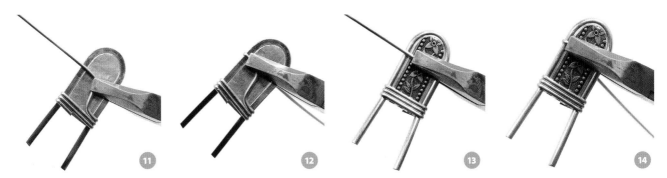

11

12

13

14

Step 5: Using flat-nose pliers, make a walk-along wrap across the back of one of the pieces **(Figures 9 through 12)**. Then finish wrapping with two more wraps across the piece, ending on the back side **(Figures 13 through 16)**. Cut the two frame wires to ⅜" (1 cm), file smooth, and form loops with the smallest step of the step-nose pliers **(Figures 17 and 18)**.

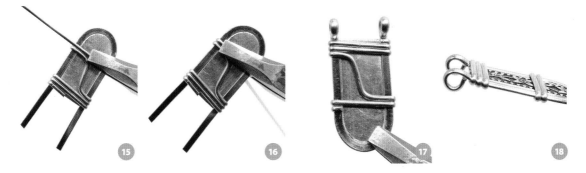

15

16

17

18

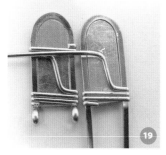

Step 6: We want the earrings to match, so compare them side by side as you add the walk-along wraps to the second earring following Steps 4 and 5 **(Figure 19)**. **Figure 20** shows a completed matching pair.

Step 7: To make hangers for the earrings, cut two pieces of the 14-gauge (1.6 mm) wire 1" (2.5 cm) long. Curve each wire, flat side down, over a dowel or step mandrel about ¼" (6 mm) in diameter **(Figure 21)**.

Step 8: Using the smallest part of round-nose or flat/round-nose pliers, curl the ends of the wires into loops **(Figure 22)**. For an additional bit of refinement, you can file the ends of the wires to a point before looping them. Curve the ends upward a little, as in **Figure 23**.

Step 9: Open the loops on each earring just enough that its hanger can be slipped through and close the loops **(Figure 24)**. This process will require a bit of adjusting.

Step 10: Make your own ear wires with coiled ends passing under the hangers, as shown in **Figure 25**, or simply attach purchased silver or gold-filled French ear wires. Use acetone or Goo-Gone to clean off any masking tape residue.

MAKE THE PENDANT

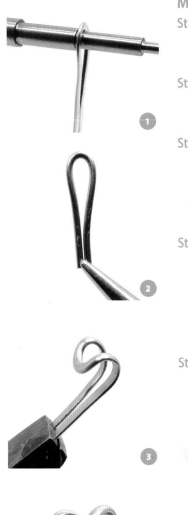

Step 1:   Repeat Steps 1 through 9 of the earrings to make a pendant for the necklace.

Step 2:   Cut and straighten a 2" (5 cm) length of the 16-gauge (1.3 mm) wire. Use a longer piece of wire if you want a longer bail.

Step 3:   Curve the wire around a dowel or step mandrel about ⅛" (3 mm) in diameter and squeeze the wires close together, as shown in **Figures 1 and 2**. Note that the wire is curved on its side with the flat and rounded sides facing front and back.

Step 4:   While holding the piece securely with flat-nose pliers, curl the piece with step-nose pliers, using the second step, which should be about ⅛" (3 mm) in diameter **(Figure 3)**. To keep the curl uniform, insert the pliers from one end, then the other, as you did while looping the clasp for the patterned bracelet.

Step 5:   Curl the end wires into loops, one at a time, using the smallest diameter on the step-nose pliers **(Figure 4)**.

Step 6:   Open the bail, slide it onto the hanger, and close it; then slide the finished pendant onto the chain of your choice **(Figure 5)**. The bail can face either direction: There is no front or back.

Now you're fully accessorized with elegant, totally customized, and completely matching earrings, pendant, and bracelet!

Variations

Turn your creative powers loose again. Vary, embellish, play.

Patterned Wire Bracelet using both broad and narrow pattern wire.

Variation of the Patterned Wire Bracelet, wrapped with half-round and twisted gold-filled wire.

Russ Sperring

Russ Sperring created the Wire-Wrapped Ring featured on page 86. He has been designing handmade jewelry for the past six years, and his work involves designing, stringing, wirework, silversmithing, and stone cutting. He also enjoys experimenting with precious metal clay and glass beadmaking.

Russ and his wife have been creating jewelry together since 2001. Dotty and Russ have four children and enjoy their country home in Morgantown, Indiana. You may contact Russ at timelessdesigns@earthlink.net.

SUPPLIERS

David H. Fell & Company Inc.
www.dhfco.com
info@dhfco.com
(800) 822-1996
(323) 722-6567 Fax
PO Box 910952
Los Angeles, CA 90091-0952
Specialties: Beautiful sterling silver patterned sheet metal, materials, and refining.

FDJ Tools
www.fdjtool.com
(800) 323-6091
(800) 634-1070
1180 Solana Ave.
Winter Park, FL 32789
Specialties: Tools, equipment, and displays.

Fire Mountain Gems & Beads
www.firemountaingems.com
(800) 355-2137 to order
(800) 423-2319 Customer Service
(800) 292-3473 Fax
One Firemountain Wy.
Grants Pass, OR 97526-2373
Specialties: Beads and gems, beading supplies.

Hoover & Strong
www.hooverandstrong.com
(800) 759-9997
10700 Trade Rd.
Richmond, VA 23236-3000
Specialties: Colored gold (white, green, pink) and an emphasis on refining your scrap metal.

Indian Jewelers Supply Company
www.ijsinc.com
orders@ijsinc.com
catalogs@ijsinc.com
(800) 545-6540
(888) 722-4175 Fax
601 E. Coal Ave.
Gallup, NM 87301
Specialties: Tools, equipment, materials, and findings.

Metalliferous
www.metalliferous.com
(212) 944-0909
(888) 944-0909
(212) 944-0644 Fax
34 West 46th St.
New York, NY 10036
Specialties: Lots of metals — niobium, aluminum, memory wire, brass, surgical steel, iron, steel, nickel, silver, and copper.

Paul H. Gesswein & Co. Inc.
www.gesswein.com
(800) 243-4466
(888) 454-4377 Fax
255 Hancock Ave.
PO Box 3998
Bridgeport, CT 06605-0936
Specialties: Tools and equipment.

Precious Metals West
www.preciousmetalswest.com
(800) 999-7528
(213) 689-1654 Fax
608 S. Hill St., Ste. #407
Los Angeles, CA 90014
Specialties: Colored alloys, sheet metal, wire, and refining.

Rio Grande (The Bell Group)
www.riogrande.com
(800) 545-6566 within the U.S.
(800) 965-2329 Fax within the U.S.
(800) 253-9738 Canada, Virgin Islands, and Puerto Rico
(505) 839-3011 for all other countries
(505) 839-3016 Fax for all other countries
7500 Bluewater Rd. NW
Albuquerque, NM 87121-1962
Specialties: Tools and equipment, materials, display products, and refining.

Ross Metals
www.rossmetals.com
(800) 654-7677
(212) 768-3018
54 West 47th St.
New York, NY 10036
Specialties: Beautiful patterned wire, alloys, wire, sheet metal, and refining.

Shor International Corporation
www.ishor.com
(914) 667-1100
(914) 667-0190 (Fax)
shorinternational@attglobal.net
20 Parkway West
Mt. Vernon, NY 10552
Specialties: You can find the wire-wrapping ring mandrel here in two sizes, plus lots of other tools and supplies.

AUTHORS

Linda's Web address is:
www.jewelrybylinda.com
Christine's Web address is:
www.christineritcheyjewelry.com
Her e-mail is:
critchey48@hotmail.com

WEBSITES

http://brandywinejewelry-supply.com
Copper and brass practice wire, half-round, round, square, etc. Also beads of all kinds, findings, packaging, and more.

www.ganoksin.com
Lurk and learn as some of the most prominent people in the jewelry business discuss every aspect of jewelry making. Most catalog companies monitor this site and you will see posts from Tiffany's, Charles Lewton-Brain, and many other luminaries in the world of jewelry. When you feel brave enough, put your question(s) before this wonderful group of experts. Beginners and beginners' questions are always answered clearly and generously. Ganoksin also has galleries of members' work as well as an extensive library of topics. Metalcalc can help you with any mathematical formula or conversion. The site was founded by Dr. E. Hanuman Aspler and Charles Lewton-Brain and survives on the donations of its generous members. Absolutely the best website for jewelry makers.

www.jewelrymaking.about.com
This site has projects and technical information related to jewelry making.

www.jewelrytoolsbymiland.com
If you can't find a specialty tool anywhere else, look here. If you still can't find what you need, this gentleman will probably make it for you.

http://www.landofodds.com/store/wire.htm
Copper and brass practice wire, even half-round!

www.lapidaryart.com
Amy O'Connell's wonderful website. Great jewelry, plus tutorials on lapidary, jewelry, and photography. Amy even tells you how she made her website.

www.snagmetalsmith.org/snag/links
Useful links provided by the highly respected SNAG organization.

www.monsterslayer.com
No print catalog, but lots of supplies, tools, materials, sterling and fine silver findings, beads, equipment, and display items.

BOOKS

Codina, Carles. *The Complete Book of Jewelry Making.* Asheville, North Carolina: Lark Books, 2000. This is a great book. Hardcover, 160 pages.

McCreight, Tim. *The Complete Metalsmith.* New York: Sterling Publishing, 1991.
This is a wonderful basic book. The companion video with the same title is invaluable for learning soldering and annealing. You can actually see the proper colors as the metal is heated and can watch the solder flow. Not available at Amazon.com, but Rio Grande has both the book and the video. Spiral-bound, 150 pages.

McGrath, Jinks. *The Encyclopedia of Jewelry Making Techniques.* Philadelphia: Running Press Books, 1995.
Hardcover, 176 pages.

Sinclair, Ellsworth. *Moods in Wire: An Extended Guided to the Fine Art of Wirewrapping, 2nd edition.* Manassas, Virginia: EE Sinclair, 2002.
Many wire wrappers learned their craft from this venerable book. Mostly black-and-white line drawings, it does have a color section in the middle. Good, basic information for the beginning wire wrapper and some nice projects for most of us. Spiral-bound soft cover, 192 pages.

Wicks, Sylvia. *Jewelry Making Manual.* Portland, Maine: Brynmorgen Press, 1990.
Hardcover, 176 pages.

MAGAZINES

Bead & Button
www.beadandbutton.com

Beadwork
www.interweave.com

Colored Stone
www.colored-stone.com

The Crafts Report
www.craftsreport.com
Covers the business issues of all crafts—very helpful.

Jewelry Crafts
www.jewelrycraftsmag.com

Jewelry Artist
www.jewelryartistmagazine.com

Metalsmith
www.snagmetalsmith.org

Ornament
No website—Call (760) 599-0222 or Fax (760) 559-0228
Gorgeous magazine—great for inspiration and ideas.

The Sunshine Artist
www.sunshineartist.com
Covers show and gallery schedules. This is a great way to find places to sell your jewelry.

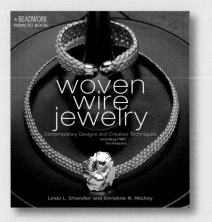
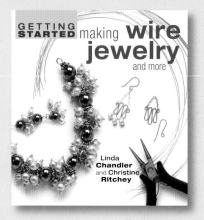